EXPLORATION IN TIBET

EXPLORATION IN TIBET

SWAMI PRANAVĀNANDA

GYAN

Published by

Gyan Publishing House
5, Ansari Road
Daryaganj, New Delhi-110002
Phone: 011-47034999, 9811692060
E-mail: books@gyanbooks.com

Distribution Network
gyanbooks.com
India, USA, Canada, UK, Australia, France

ISBN : 978-81-212-9632-8 (PB)
First Published, 1939

2nd Impression 2023

Printed at: Gyan Press, Delhi.

EXPLORATION IN TIBET
Author: SWAMI PRANAVANANDA

Swami Pranavānanda (of the Holy Kailas and Manasarovar)

EXPLORATION IN TIBET

SWAMI PRANAVĀNANDA

(OF THE HOLY KAILAS AND MANASAROVAR)

1939

DEDICATED

To

THE HON'BLE RAI BAHADUR LALA RAMA SARAN DAS,

C.I.E., M.C.S.,

of Lahore,

with Love and Admiration

for the interest he has taken in the

Author's tour to the

HOLY KAILAS and MANASAROVAR

on various occasions.

CONTENTS

PART I

A Twelve-month on the Holy Kailas and Manasarovar

Mount Kailas and Lake Manasarovar

CHAPTER I

CHAPTER II

CHAPTER III

CHAPTER VIII

CHAPTER IV

ILLUSTRATIONS

MAPS

(At the end of the book)

PREFACE

"*Search for the truth is the noblest occupation of man; its publication is a duty.*"

"I revelled in the consciousness that except the Tibetans themselves, no other human beings but myself had penetrated to this spot......Not without pride, but still with a feeling of humble thankfulness, I stood there, conscious that I was the first white man who has ever penetrated to the source of the Indus and Brahmaputra." Thus declared Dr. Sven Hedin in 1908 in his 'Trans-Himalaya.' Since then, the entire Geographical world believed that his was the last word on the subject of 'The Sources of the Four Great Rivers of the Holy Kailas and Manasarovar.'

Thirty years had elasped before it fell to the lot of a humble Indian Swami in the person of the author unaided by any of the essential modern equipment for exploration, to find out certain discrepancies and errors in the findings of Sven Hedin. Herein lies the explanation for bringing out the present work; for to discover Nature's Secrets, to realise Truth, and to disseminate knowledge are as much the duty and privilege of a spiritual aspirant as of a scientist.

On account of the wide spiritual appeal of Mount Kailas and Lake Manasarovar, and the exquisite beauty and grandeur of the entire neighbouring region, the author thinks fit to give a rather elaborate account in the first part of this monograph. In presenting this volume to the public he wishes to draw the attention of the reader to the fact that when he visited Calcutta in 1938, his work was appreciated by Dr. Shibaprasad Chatterjee, M.Sc., Ph.D. (Lond.), D.Litt. (Paris), F.G.S., Lecturer-in-Charge of Geography, Calcutta University, and a word of encouragement was also given by the Surveyor-General of India and the Director of Map Publication Department. The subject-matter of the book comprises of the two papers read before the Calcutta Geographical Society. A brief note on the subject was also published in the *Journal* of the Royal Geographical Society, London, for February, 1939. A summary of the paper on the sources of the rivers was also read in the Geography Section of the 26th Session of the Indian Science Congress Association, held at Lahore in January, 1939.

With a view to obviating the necessity of consulting Sven Hedin's works constantly on the part of the reader in following the points of dispute, and elucidating the arguments, no hesitation has been felt in giving lengthy quotations. As referred to in the text, the author had been to the Kailas-Manasarovar area altogether four times and on each occasion proceeded systematically to explore the sources, resolving doubts, if any, pertaining to materials collected on the previous tour. Throughout this enquiry, he has always kept only one aim in the forefront namely, to leave nothing shrouded in mystery nor give room for speculation.

The author thinks fit to append the glossary of translation of a few Tibetan and other words which are used in the body of the book. He has also given two maps with eight insets to enable the reader to follow the discussion in full, obviating any difficulty and confusion that might otherwise arise in absence of these. The author considers his labour to have not gone in vain if the book succeeds in inducing even a few readers to undertake an expedition and throw further light by way of confirmation of the author's topography and hydrography of the Kailas-Manasarovar region.

It is with the greatest pleasure that the author takes this opportunity of expressing his very hearty thanks to Dr. Shibaprasad Chatterjee for the encouragement he has given him and the keen interest he has taken in discussing the subject, but for which the work would not have seen the light of day so soon. The author desires to express his grateful thanks to Dr. Syamaprasad Mookerjee, M.A., B.L., D.Litt., Barrister-at-Law, M.L.A., Ex-Vice-Chancellor of the Calcutta University, and to Mr. J. C. Chakravorti, M.A., Registrar, for the kind interest they have taken in the new discoveries embodied in the book and giving publicity to them. The author expresses his gratitude and thanks to Brevet-Colonel L. H. Jackson, I.A., the Surveyor-General of India, and to Lt.-Colonel O. Slater, M.C., R.E., the Director of Map Publication Department, Survey of India and to Mr. M. Mahadevan, M.A., the Superintendent, for their courtesy and kindness in incorporating the recent observations and corrections pointed out by the author, into the latest maps with the various insets, and for getting them prepared and printed for him in the Survey Office; and also to Captain C. A. K. Wilson, R.E., Photo-Litho Office for expediting the printing of the maps. The author further tenders his love and affection to his friends Messrs. A. Jogarao, M.Sc., and S. Raju, M.Sc. of the Department of Chemistry, Benares Hindu University, for helpful criticism offered and suggestions given in the preparation of the volume; and to Mr. Dinabandhu Ganguli, B.A., Superintendent, Calcutta University Press for having attended to the prompt publication of the book. The author's affectionate thanks are due to Shree Bhupendra Nath Sinha, Raja Saheb of Barwari (Bhagalpur) who defrayed the major portion of the expenses for his stay on Manasarovar for a year and for his visits to the sources of the Four Great Rivers; and also to Srimans Keshab Mohan Thakur and Suraj Mohan Thakur, Zemindars of Barari Estate and to the several other friends who helped him financially and otherwise, for the undertaking of his travels to the Holy Kailas and Manasarovar region in Tibet on various occasions.

CALCUTTA,
August, 1939.

SWAMI PRANAVANANDA
(of the Holy Kailas and Manasarovar)

EXPLORATION IN TIBET

PART I

A TWELVE-MONTH ON THE HOLY KAILAS AND LAKE MANASAROVAR

1. Northern View of Mount Kailas [*See page 1*

ॐ

CHAPTER I

Mount Kailas and Lake Manasarovar

Two hundred and forty miles from Almora in U. P. and 800 miles from Lhasa, the capital of Tibet, stands Mount Kailas with Lake Manasarovar constituting one of the grandest of the Himalayan beauty spots. The perpetual snow-clad peak of the Holy Kailas (styled *Kang Rinpochhe* in the Tibetan language) of hoary antiquity and celebrity, the spotless design of Nature's art, of most bewitching and overpowering beauty, has a vibration of the supreme order from the spiritual point of view. It seems to stand as an immediate revelation of the Almighty in concrete form, which makes man kneel down and bow his head in reverence. Its gorgeous silvery summit, resplendent with the lustre of spiritual aura, pierces into a heavenly height of 22,028 feet above the level of the even bosom of the sea. The *parikrama* or circumambulation of the *Kailas Parvat* is about 32 miles. There are five Buddhist monasteries (*gompas*)* around it singing, year in and year out, the glory of the Buddha, the Enlightened, and his five hundred *Bodhisattvas*, said to be seated on the top of the Sacred Peak of

* Also pronounced 'gonpa.'

Kailas. Mount Kailas is reverenced in Sanskrit literature as the abode of the All-blissful Lord Shiva, which from 20 miles off is overlooking the Holy Manasarovar and the Rakshas Tal bedecked with graceful swans, on the south.

The Holy Manasarovar, the *Tso Mapham* or *Tso Mavang* of the Tibetans, is the holiest, the most fascinating, the most inspiring, and the most famous of all the lakes in the world and the most ancient that civilization knows. "Manasarowar was the first lake known to geography. Lake Manasarowar is famous in Hindu mythology; it had in fact become famous many centuries before the lake of Geneva had aroused any feeling of admiration in civilized man. Before the dawn of history Manasarowar had become the sacred lake and such it has remained for four millennium."* She is majestically calm and dignified like a huge bluish green emerald or a pure turquoise set between the two mighty and equally majestic silvery mountains, the Kailas on the north and the Gurla Mandhata on the south and between the sister-lake Rakshas Tal or Ravan Hrad (*Langak Tso* of the Tibetans) on the west and some hills on the east. Her heaving bosom, reflecting the resplendent golden rays of the waning sun and the myriad pleasant hues of the vesper sky, or her smooth surface mirroring the amber columns or silvery beams of the rising sun or moon, adds a mystic charm, all her own, to the already mysteriously charming Lake. From the

* S. G. Burrard and H. H. Hayden, 'A sketch of the geography and geology of the Himalaya mountains and Tibet,' Delhi, Survey of India (1934), Part III, p. 228.

2. Sunrise on Lake Manasarovar [*See page 2*

spiritual point of view, she has a most enrapturing vibration of the supremest order that can soothe and lull even the most wandering mind into sublime serenity and can transport it into involuntary ecstacies.* Stretching majestically over an extensive cradle of the Tibetan plateau and hanging at a heavenly height of 14,950 feet above the sea-level, the vast expanse of the Lake, with a circumference of about 54 miles and a depth of nearly 300 feet, covers an area of 200 square miles. There stand eight monasteries on the holy shores, wherein Buddhist monks strive all their lives to attain the sublimity of the eternal silence of *Nirvana*.

In order to realise and appreciate fully the grandeur of the Holy Lake, one has actually to spend at least a twelve-month on her shores. For those who have not even paid her a casual visit, it would be difficult, if not impossible, to imagine the diverse aspects of beauty that she presents through the different seasons of the year to closer observers. By far the most magnificent and thrilling of one's experiences would be in winter when the entire Lake freezes hard, and again in spring when she breaks in and melts into clear blue waters. It is only the inspired poet or divine artist who can describe and represent adequately the beauty and grandeur of sunrise and sunset on the Lake.

The actual circumference of Manasarovar is about 54 miles at the most and never 200 or 80 miles

* For a fuller treatment o the subject read the author's pamphlet *Spiritual Vibration*.

as the Japanese Buddhist monk Ekai Kawaguchi (who travelled in Tibet for three years) and some other casual visitors, who themselves never undertook the circuit of the Lake, would ask us to believe. Out of my nine circumambulations of the Holy Manas, I did some in four days, some in three days and one in two days. Skull-like, the Lake is much broader in the north than in the south. The east, south, west, and north coasts of the Lake are roughly 16, 10, 13 and 15 miles in length respectively. The *parikrama* of Manasarovar visiting all the eight monasteries is about 64 miles. Tibetans do the *parikrama* (called *kora*) of the Holy Lake in winter when the entire surface of the Lake and all the rivers and streams flowing into it are frozen, so that they might go throughout along the shores; or in early winter or spring when most of the smaller streams are dry and the bigger ones contain less water so as to be easily fordable. In the summer and rainy seasons, one cannot go along the shores throughout. On the northern side one shall have to leave the shores and go higher up. Moreover, all the streams and rivers flowing into the Lake will be in high floods in summer due to melting snow and would be flowing very furiously, which oftentimes become unfordable after midday. On such occasions one has to stop for the night and wait till the next morning for low-tide. Moreover, at the time when Indian pilgrims visit Kailas and the Manas, the shores of the Lake are much frequented by nomad robber tribes going up and down. Those who want to go round the Holy Lake in summer or rainy season, should do so in parties guarded by armed men and they should take good ponies or yaks to cross the rapid rivers on.*

Orthodox Tibetans take 3 or 13 rounds of the Kailas and the Manas and some of the more pious pilgrims do the *sashtanga-danda-pradakshina* (prostration circuit) of Manasarovar in about 28 days and of Kailas in 15 days. Several Tibetans do the *parikrama* of Kailas in a single day which is called *chhokar.* Some rich and sick people who cannot do the *parikrama* themselves engage beggars or coolies to do the circumambulations of the Kailas or Manasarovar and pay some remuneration besides provisions for the laborious undertaking. It is believed that one *parikrama* of the Kailas peak washes off the sin of one life, 10 circuits wash off the sin of one *kalpa*, and 108 *parikramas* secure *Nirvana* in this very life.

The eight monasteries round Manasarovar are : (1) Gossul gompa (west), (2) Chiu gompa (N.W.), (3) Cherkip gompa (N.), (4) Langpona gompa (N.), (5) Ponri gompa (N.), (6) Seralung gompa (E.), (7) Yerngo gompa (S.), and (8) Thugolho gompa† or Thokar (S.). There are four *lings* or *chhortens* (memorials of some great lamas) and four *chhak-chhal-gangs* (wherefrom *sashtanga-danda-pranamam* or prostration salute is made) round Manasarovar. The four *chhortens* are at Chiu

* For fuller details of the pilgrimage, one can refer to the author's *Pilgrims' Companion to the Holy Kailas and Manasarovar*, published by Rai Saheb Ram Dayal Agarwala, Allahabad.

† It is in this monastery that the author lived for one year

gompa, Langpona gompa, Seralung gompa, and Thugolho gompa. The four *chhak-chhal-gangs* are at Momo donkhang (S.W.), Sera la (W.), Havasenimadang (E.), and Riljung (S.E.).

The five monasteries of Kailas are (1) Nyanri or Chhuku gompa (W.), (2) Diraphuk gompa (N.), (3) Zunthulphuk gompa (E.), (4) Gengta gompa (S.), and (5) Silung gompa* (S.). There are four *shapjes* or footprints of the Buddha, four *chaktaks* or chains, and four *chhak-chhal-gangs*, round Kailas. There is a big flag-staff called *tarbochhe* at Sershung on the western side of Kailas. A big fair is held there on *Vaisakha Sukla Chaturdasi* and *Purnima* (full-moon day in the month of May), when the old flag-staff is dug out and re-hoisted with new flags, that full-moon day being the day of birth, Enlightenment, and *Nirvana* of Lord Buddha. Situated on the eastern side of the Kailas peak is Gourikund, called Thuki Zingboo by Tibetans. It is a small beautiful oval-shaped lake covered with sheets of ice almost all the year round. The descent of avalanches into the lake from the southern heights is rather a frequent occurrence. On the southern foot of the Mount is Tso Kapala.

Kangri Karchhak—the Tibetan *Kailas Purana*—says, that Kailas is in the centre of the whole universe towering right up into the sky like the handle of a mill-stone, that half-way on its side is *Kalpa Vriksha* (wish-fulfilling tree), that it has square sides of gold and jewels, that the eastern face is crystal, the southern sapphire, the western

* Also pronounced 'Serlung.'

ruby, and the northern gold, that the peak is clothed in fragrant flowers and herbs, that there are four footprints of the Buddha on the four sides so that Kailas might not be taken away into the sky by the deities of that region and four chains so that the denizens of the lower regions might not take it down.

The presiding deity of Kailas is Demchhok, also called Pavo. He puts on tiger skins and garlands of human skulls and holds *damaru* (vibrant drum) in one hand and *khatam* (trident) in the other. Round Kailas are some more deities sitting in 990 rows with 500 in each. All these also put on tiger skins, etc., like Demchhok. By the side of Demchhok is a female deity called Khando or Ekajati. Besides these Lord Buddha and his 500 Bodhisattvas are said to be residing on the Kailas. At the foot of the sacred peak is seated Hanumanju, the monkey-god. There are also the abodes of several more deities around the Kailas and Manasarovar. All these deities could be seen only by the pious few. Sounds of bells, cymbals, and other musical instruments are heard on the top of Kailas.

There are seven rows of trees round the Holy Manasarovar, and there is a big mansion in it, in which resides the king of *Nags* (serpent-gods) and the surface of the Lake is arc-like with a huge tree in the middle. The fruits of the tree fall into the Lake with the sound *jam ;* so the surrounding region of the earth is named 'Jambu-ling,' the Jambudwipa of Hindu *Puranas*. Some of the fruits that fall into the Lake are eaten by the *Nags* and the rest become gold and sink down to the bottom.

The scripture further says, that the four great rivers called (1) the Langchen Khambab or the Elephant-mouthed river (Sutlej) on the west, (2) the Singi Khambab or the Lion-mouthed river (Indus) on the north, (3) the Tamchok Khambab or the Horse-mouthed river (Brahmaputra) on the east, and (4) the Mapcha Khambab or Peacock-mouthed river (Karnali) on the south, have their sources in Tso Mapham—the Lake unconquerable (Manasarovar); that the water of the Sutlej is cool, the water of the Indus hot, the water of the Brahmaputra cold, and of the Karnali warm; and that there are sands of gold in the Sutlej, sands of diamonds in the Indus, sands of emeralds in the Brahmaputra, and sands of silver in the Karnali. It is also said that these four rivers circle seven times round Kailas and Manasarovar and then take their courses towards west, north, east, and south respectively.

According to the Tibetan traditions and scriptures, the source of the Sutlej is in the springs near Dulchu* gompa, about 30 miles west of Manasarovar; the source of the Indus is in the springs of Singi Khambab, north-east of Kailas, about 62 miles from Manasarovar; the source of the Brahmaputra is in the Chema-yungdung glaciers, about 63 miles south-east of Manasarovar; and the source of the Karnali is in the spring Mapcha Chungo, about 30 miles south-west of Manasarovar. The sources of these four rivers are within a distance of about 45 miles (as the crow flies) from the shores of the Holy Lake. So the description of the Tibetan scriptures

* Also pronounced 'Dunchu.'

that these four rivers take their sources from Kailas and Manasarovar is not far from the truth, also because the author of the *Kangri Karchhak* must certainly have taken Kailas and Manasarovar including the area surrounding them extending up to the sources of these rivers as 'Kailas-Manasarovar region.' It is on this score that I would like to call the region surrounding Kailas and Manasarovar, extending up to the river Chhinku on the west, the source of the Indus on the north, the source of the Brahmaputra on the east, and the Indian borders on the south, as 'Kailas-Manasarovar region' or simply 'Manasarovar region' or 'Manasa Khanda.'

Since the advent of Aryan civilization into India, Tibet and especially the Kailas-Manasarovar region have been glorified in the Hindu mythology as part of the Himalayas. The *Ramayana* and the *Mahabharata,* all the *Puranas* in general and *Manasakhanda* of *Skanda Purana* in particular sing the glory of Manasarovar. She is the creation of the *manas* (mind) of Brahma, the first of the Trinity of the Hindu mythology; and according to some the Maharaja Mandhata found out the Manasarovar. Mandhata is said to have done penance on the shores of Manasarovar at the foot of the mountains which are now known after his name. In some Pali and Sanskrit Buddhist works, Manasarovar is described as *Anavatapta*—lake without heat and trouble. In the centre is a tree which bears fruits that are 'omnipotent' in healing all human ailments, physical as well as mental, and as such much sought after by gods and men alike. This *Anavatapta* is described as the only true paradise on earth. It is also said that mighty lotuses, as big as the Amitabha Buddha, bloom in the Holy Lake, and the Buddha and the Bodhisattvas often sit on those flowers. Heavenly *Rajahansas* will be singing their celestial melodies as they swim on the Lake. On the surrounding mountains of the Lake are found the *shata-mulikas* or hundred herbs.

At a distance of 1½ to 6 miles to the west of Manasarovar is the Rakshas Tal, also known as Ravan Hrad, Rakshas Sarovar, or Ravan Sarovar where Ravana of Lanka fame was said to have done penance to propitiate Lord Shiva, the third of the Hindu Trinity and the dweller of Kailas. There goes a story in Tibetan scriptures about the Rakshas Tal and the Ganga Chhu, the outlet of Manas into the Rakshas. Rakshas Tal was originally the abode of demons; as such nobody drank water out of it. Two golden fish that were in the Manas fought against each other and one pursued the other into Rakshas Tal. The course which the golden fish took then is the present course of the Ganga Chhu. When the holy waters of the Manas flowed out through the course of the golden fish into Rakshas Tal, the latter became sanctified. From that time onwards, people began to drink the water of Rakshas Tal. I took nine rounds of the Holy Manasarovar and found Ganga Chhu to be the only outlet, which is 40 to 100 feet in breadth. So the statement and belief of several people, who had never made even one full circuit of Manasarovar, that the Brahmaputra and the Indus take their rise on the eastern and northern banks respectively, are absolutely groundless and erroneous like the statements that the Indus has its source at the northern or southern foot of Kailas peak and flows on its western or southern side, and that the Sutlej takes its rise in Gourikund and flows on the eastern side of Kailas.

There are two islands in Rakshas Tal, one Lachato and the other Topserma (or Dopserma). I visited these islands on April 15 and 16, 1937, when the lake was completely frozen. I went over the frozen lake from east to west and from south to north on a yak. Lachato is a rocky and hilly island having the appearance of a tortoise with the neck stretched out towards a peninsula on the southern shore. The distance between the neck of the island and the cape of the peninsula is about half a mile. The circumference of the island is nearly one mile. On the top of the hill is a *laptche*, a heap of stones, with *mani*-slabs. On the western and eastern sides of the hill there are walled enclosures of egg-gatherers. There were several swans (or wild geese as some might like to call them) on the level ground of the eastern side of the island. The egg-gatherers of the *goba* (headman) of the village Kardung were expected there in the last week of April, when the swans would begin to lay eggs.

Two accidents that had occurred in Rakshas Tal several years ago were narrated to me by an old Tibetan. One night when two egg-gatherers were on the Lachato, Rakshas Tal broke in all of a sudden and they were stranded on the island. They had to live on what little provisions they had with them, on the flesh of the few hares that were on the island, and on the eggs of swans; they remained on the island till the lake froze in the next winter, enabling them to reach the mainland. But they were very much emaciated for want of sufficient food and one of them succumbed to it a few days after. Nobody had the idea of making a small skin boat or a raft to bring the stranded men to the mainland. On another occasion, in early spring, when a fully loaded yak was crossing the lake, the ice under its feet gave way and it sank down under its own weight.

Topserma, the second island, is completely rocky and hilly like the Lachato but much bigger. Its southern part is named Tumuk. The island is about a mile from east to west and about three-fourths of a mile from north to south. On the eastern projection of the hill is a *pucca*-walled house in ruins, in which a Khampa Lama was said to have lived for seven years some time ago. He used to come out of the island to the shores in winter after the freezing of the lake to take provisions. I picked up a small clay-made image of *Chenresi* (Avalokiteswara) from the ruins, as a memento of my visit to the island. I am the first non-Tibetan who has ever stood on the tops of the hills on these two islands in Rakshas Tal. Down below the projection there are two or three camping walled enclosures. Topserma is under the jurisdiction of the *goba* of Shungba. There were no aquatic birds on this island when I visited it.

In the maps of Dr. Sven Hedin and of the Survey of India office, three islands are shown in Rakshas Tal, although the names of only two of them are given. Further, this third island

and Topserma are drawn in broken lines. From my personal observation and information I found only two islands in the Rakshas Tal. If there is a third island at all, it must have been completely hidden under snow, when I went over the lake in winter. I went round the Rakshas Tal leaving the south-western and north-western parts. Secondly, the *goba* of the Rakshas Tal area got his house constructed about the year 1930, within three miles from the island Topserma, which is under his jurisdiction. He too says that there are only two islands in the Rakshas Tal. Thirdly, in August, 1938, I procured a water-colour painting of the Kailas-Manasarovar region drawn by a late monk of the famous Similing monastery of Taklakot, which has a branch monastery, Tsapgye, on the west coast of Rakshas Tal. The monk must, therefore, have surely got an intimate knowledge of the Rakshas Tal. He has shown only two islands in the Rakshas Tal in his painting. Lastly, when Sven Hedin went round the Rakshas Tal he had with him local Tibetan guides, who doubtless would have given him the name of the third island also, if it had been there. It is, therefore, evident that both the maps are doubtful about the existence of the third island and about the correct position of Topserma; yet they show the third island also. That Sven Hedin himself has no definite knowledge about these islands can be seen from the following: "The two islands are easily visible in the south-western corner of the lake, but one can only seldom make out that they are real islands and not parts of promontories. There may possibly be three of them. The greatest is called Dopserma, though other Tibetans called (*sic*) Dotser."*

The climate of Kailas-Manasarovar region in particular and of Tibet in general is very cold, dry, and windy. Monsoon sets in late and rainfall is scanty; but when it rains it does in torrents. In summer all streams and rivers flow very rapidly and sometimes become unfordable in the evenings, due to melting snow The sun is pretty hot in summer but it becomes very cold as soon as the sky gets cloudy. During the pilgrim season (July and August), very often the Holy Kailas and the Mandhata peaks would be enveloped in clouds and be playing hide-and-seek with the visitors. During the cloudy part of a day and during nights it would be very cold. There will be tempestuous winds from the beginning of November up to the middle of May. Weather changes like the weather-cock. Now you will be perspiring profusely in the hot sun; in a few minutes cool breezes gently blow; the next moment you will have clouds witb terrific thunders and lightnings followed by drizzling or downpours of water in torrents; sometimes you will see a rainbow; shortly after you may have a hail-storm followed by showers of snowfall. Here is bright sun; a little further away a shower of rain; and further up lashing rains. Here is perfect calmness; the next moment there break out whizzing tempestuous winds. Now you are on the top of a mountain in the bright sun; below, you see columns of clouds rising like smoke; and further down it is raining.

* Sven Hedin, 'Southern Tibet,' Vol. II, p. 167.

Here on a conical peak the ice is glittering in the sun like a bar of silver; there on a dome-like peak are hanging golden canopies; the far-off mountain ranges are enveloped in thick wreaths of inky black clouds; there appears a belt of amber clouds or the seven-coloured semi-circular rainbow encircles the Kailas Dome; or the near-by Mandhata's giant hoods are ablaze in scarlet flames when the sun begins to dip in the west; or the meagre snow-clad Ponri peak raises its head into the pitch-dark messengers of Indra. Here in front of you the rising sun pours forth molten gold on the azure expanse of the enchanting Lake, throwing you into a deep spell; there a far-off valley gives out thick fumes of sulphur under peculiar weather conditions, indicating the presence of big thermal springs. From one side warm winds give you a good welcome and from another valley shivering cold blasts attack you. Sometimes it seems that day and night, morning, noon and evening, and all the six seasons of the year have their sway simultaneously.

CHAPTER II

FREEZING OF MANASAROVAR

When I was on the shores of Manasarovar in 1936-37, winter had already begun to make itself felt from the middle of September. From October 1 onward up to May 14, 1937, the minimum temperature persistently remained below the freezing point. The maximum temperature during that year was 67°F. on July 19, in the verandah of my room and the minimum was −18·5°F. on February 18, when the sputum of a person standing on the balcony would become solid before it reaches the ground. The lowest maximum temperature was 2°F. on February 16. The maximum temperature remained below the freezing point for nearly 3½ months; and on several occasions even at noon the temperature would be −10°F. Of course the winter of 1936-37 was unusually severe in the Kailas-Manasarovar region.

Occasional snowfalls began from the second week of September, but never were they more than 1½ feet on the shores of Manasarovar, although around Kailas there were several feet of heavy snowfall. Tempestuous winds began to howl in an ever-increasing manner from the first of November. From the middle of December, water near the edges of the Lake began to freeze to a width of two feet.

3. Gurla Mandhata Peaks [*See pages* 2, 9

4. Raising of *Tarbochhe* (flag-staff) near Kailas [*See page* 6

5. Gourikund (Thuki Zingbco) [*See page* 6

6. Avalanche descending from Mount Kailas

From the 21st, water towards the middle of the Lake froze here and there to a thickness of 2 to 4 inches and sheets of ice about 50 to 100 yards in edge were drifting towards the shores. Cyclonic gales from the Mandhata peaks were giving rise to huge oceanic waves in the Lake, which were roaring and thundering aloud. Lamas and other Tibetans were foretelling that the Lake would freeze in her entirety on the full-moon day of the month of *Margasirsha*.

It was Monday, December 28, 1936. Somehow that day, I came out of my meditation unusually at 7 A.M., I cannot say why, and looked around; it was all like the dead of night, absolutely silent and perfectly calm. Curious to know as to what had happened I went to the terrace of the monastery and stood up, and in an instant felt a thrill and lost all physical consciousness for some time—how long I cannot exactly tell. As I regained consciousness, I was stunned by the sight of the Holy Kailas on the N.W., piercing into the blue sky and dyed in amber robes of the early morning sun (which had not yet reached other places) and overlooking the Holy Lake in all majesty and dignity, bewitching even the inanimate creation. Not even a single sheep or lamb in the sheep-yard bleated. While I was musing over the splendour and overpowering beauty of the Holy Mount, it rapidly changed several robes of various colours and hues and ultimately decided upon the usual perpetual silver garment, which was reflecting in the clear and calm blue mirror of the mid-Lake. Dazzled at the sight, I lowered my eyes towards the

Lake, that was just in front of me. The very first sight of the Holy Lake made me forget myself and even the Lake herself for some time, and by the time I could see the Lake again, the sun was sufficiently high on the eastern horizon. For over a mile from the shores, the waters in the Lake were frozen into milk-white ice all around. It was an unforgettable and memorable sight—the middle of the Lake picturesquely with its unfrozen deep blue waters quite calm and serene, reflecting the Kailas and the snowy cap of the Ponri peak and the resplendent rays of the morning sun. Oh! how happy I was! I utterly fail to describe the bliss I enjoyed and the mystic charm of the enchanting Lake. There was pin-drop silence everywhere. Like the eternal silence of *Nirvana* there was perfect stillness all around. What creature could there be on the face of earth which would not feel and become one with that sublime serenity of silence of the Almighty? I leaned against the parapet of the terrace and stood dumb—struck by the most enrapturing splendour and lustre of the sublime serenity of the spiritual aura of the two holiest places on the face of the earth. How fortunate I felt myself to be under such a wonderful spell! At about 10 A.M. I was roused by the hailing shouts of the villagers. The whole village was on the house-tops, hoisting coloured flags, burning incense and hailing the gods aloud *So*! *So*!! *So*!!! There had descended a thorough change in the whole atmosphere (both physical and mental and spiritual) and I felt as if I was in an altogether new world. By December 30, *i.e.*, in full three days, the entire surface of the Lake was frozen like the mythological ocean of curds. But curiously enough Sven Hedin in his 'Trans-Himalaya' reports that the whole of Manasarovar freezes over in an hour !*

From January 1, occasional sounds and rumblings began to be heard now and then and from the 7th they became more disturbing and terrible for about a month, as if the Lake was reluctant and resisting to put on the white robe. These sounds subsided to a great extent as the severity of winter increased, perhaps indicating her assent for some time, but were heard again intensely in early spring before the breaking of the Lake. About a month after the Lake and her feeders froze (excepting at the mouths of the Ding tso and the Tag, and near Chiu gompa), I found that the level of the water in the Lake fell down by over 12 inches below the ice, which, consequently, under its own weight cracked with tremendous sounds and fissures were formed. The level of the water in the Lake must have fallen down still further, later on in winter, which I could not note and record. These fissures or chasms which are 3 to 6 feet broad partition the entire Lake, so to speak, into a number of divisions or compartments. Within 2 or 3 days, the water in the fissures freezes again and breaks with the result that slabs and blocks of ice pile up to a height of six feet. Sometimes those slabs and blocks pile up loosely over the chasms and sometimes they are cemented to either side of the fissure. Such kinds of fissures and eruptions are also formed along the shores just

* (1910) Vol. II, p. 180.

near the edges or a few feet inside the Lake; and these I name 'coastal eruptions' in contradistinction to the main fissures in the Lake. Later on, when the Lake melts in the month of May, it breaks along these fissures. The disturbance beneath the ice, due to hot springs in the bed, may also be the cause of cracks, sounds and huge fissures in Manasarovar.

Afraid of the cracks and sounds and also on account of the danger of going down into the Lake due to explosions and fissures (called *mayur* in Tibetan) none dares go on the frozen Manas even on foot. Inspite of the warnings given to me by the monks, I went over the Lake for more than a mile in order to cross it from Chiu to Cherkip gompa. All of a sudden I was face to face with a big fissure-eruption with blocks of ice loosely piled up to a height of 5 feet. As I was unprepared for the situation I had to cross the fissure at a great risk and with utmost difficulty. Before reaching Cherkip I had to cross one more fissure-eruption and one coastal eruption. At that time I was reminded of the line that "The greatest pleasure in life lies in doing what people say you cannot do" (Bagehot). But if one is well equipped, one can cross the frozen Lake in the early hours of the day in mid-winter.

It is different with the Rakshas Tal. Loaded sheep, yaks and ponies and even men on horse-back cross the frozen Rakshas Tal from east to west and from south to north. The absence of major fissures and eruptions here may be due to the fact that the water that percolates out of it by subterranean paths is being compensated for by the supply of water into it from its eastern neighbour, the Manas, through underground waterways. There is no appreciable void created beneath the ice between it and the water in the Rakshas Tal and hence perhaps there are not many fissures and eruptions in it. There are no doubt a good many coastal explosions and eruptions and a few minor fissures here and there. I actually crossed two small fissures (one foot broad) while visiting the islands in the Lake on April 15 and 16, 1937. I was, however, told by an old Tibetan that rarely, once in 8 or 10 years, a good number of fissures make their appearance even on the frozen Rakshas Tal. Both the Manas and Rakshas freeze into pure white opaque ice in the beginning and within a month or so it becomes transparent greenish blue. The thickness of the frozen ice ranges from 2 to 6 feet near the banks, as far as my observation goes.

A series of peculiar phenomena takes place on the frozen Lake of Manasarovar which it is impossible to describe fully. In one corner towards the south of the Nimapendi, the ice on the Lake cracks, and innumerable glassy panes of ice 2 to 4 tenths of an inch in thickness are hurled out into heaps in a minute as if by magic. From Thugolho to Tseti tso, due to coastal explosions huge blocks of ice 20 to 50 cubic feet in volume get hurled and cast ashore to distances ranging up to 60 feet; some of which take nearly a month to melt away, after the breaking of the Lake. Due to coastal explosions blocks of ice 3 to 4 feet thick rise like embankments 10 to 21 feet broad and 6 to 9 feet high, continuously for distances of hundreds of yards, only to collapse suddenly like so many packs of cards, on some evening, due to waves of quakes caused by subterranean disturbances, startling and confounding the *kora*-pilgrims, who might be moving slowly along the shores, unmindfully telling their prayers on the beads of the rosaries. These blocks of ice are irregular in shape from Thugolho to Yushup tso and regular up to Gossul. From Gossul to Tseti tso there are piles of perfectly plane slabs 1 to 2 inches in thickness. From Tseti tso to the volcanic rock-projection of Malla Thak there are irregular heaps of ice mixed with the shore-drifted soft water-reeds. At the Malla Thak, at the mouth of the Gyuma chhu and at some other places water is frozen into crystal-clear transparent greenish blue ice, right down to the bottom, exhibiting the pebbles, sands, and water-reeds, and the active live fish in the depths of the Lake, as through the glass cases in an aquarium. A quarter of a mile beyond the volcanic rock-projection, about 50 yards from the shore, there was an oval patch of water 30 feet in diameter in the frozen Lake, on January 28, when the minimum temperature in the verandah of my room was 2°F. and when the entire Lake was covered with ice 2 to 6 feet thick. Two scores of some aquatic birds, but not swans, were merrily swimming and playing in the pool and on the ice near-by. This makes me conclusively believe that there must be some hot springs in the bed of the Manasarovar. On the south of this pool of water two scores of birds were frozen alive and sandwiched in the Lake. For about 2½ miles from here the surface of the Lake is almost plain, with some blocks of ice here and there, and then up to Chang Donkhang there are huge blocks of all types. From Chang Donkhang up to the mouth of the Gyuma chhu, there is a series of parallel banks of white opaque ice, one foot high and three feet apart and running into the Lake for half a mile like the furrows in a potato field. These parallel banks make an angle of about 50° with the shore towards the S.E. At the mouth of the Gyuma chhu hundreds of fish, big and small, are frozen to death in a swimming posture, which could be seen clearly through the transparent ice. From the Gyuma chhu to Sham tso there are fine models of regular mountain ranges with peaks, valleys, passes and tablelands, all of opaque white ice not exceeding eight feet in height. In one of the rounds of the Lake I mused myself like a school-boy for full two hours in these ranges to find out the likeness of the various peaks of the Himalayas. I could find in these ranges varieties of peaks—pyramidal, conical, tetrahedronal, trapezoidal, slant, steep, wedge-shaped, hood-like, wall-like, spade-like, club-like and so on—though not in the same order as in the Himalayas and other ranges. From Sham tso up to the mouth of Gugta, it is a vast field of ice with marks exactly resembling the hoofs of yaks and horses, as in a rice-field made ready for plantation by several bullocks. As a matter of fact, in my first winter *parikrama* of the Holy Lake I mistook them for the footprints of wild horses and yaks. There is water almost all the year round at the mouth of the Gugta; for a mile beyond that place, one sees beautiful formations of ice, like coral reefs.

From here up to Thugo could be seen all varieties of formations and eruptions without any special features at any particular place, excepting at the mouth of the Nimapendi. Mostly between the mouths of the Gyuma and the Tag, all along the edge of the Lake, there is a fine foot-path of ice 6 to 10 feet broad where beginners can practise skating and where I used to slide on merrily.

Besides these, I would just mention a few more interesting features of the frozen Manas and then proceed to the breaking of the Lake. Now and then the ice on the Lake bursts forth and fountains of water gush out and small pools are formed temporarily on the ice, only to be frozen hard during the night; but such pools formed in early spring are of bigger dimensions and do not freeze again to welcome the early-coming adventurous pairs of swans. In some corner, thousands of white needles and pins, flowers and creepers of various designs form under and over the transparent greenish blue ice. Occasionally one sees several regularly-beaten white foot-paths and lines on the entire surface of the transparent Lake, which vanish also in a night in an equally mysterious way. These may be termed ' miniature fissures,' though there are no chasms. When the Lake breaks, the bigger sheets of ice collide with one another and split up into smaller pieces along these paths and lines. Sometimes it is one white sheet of ice from edge to edge and sometimes the whole Lake becomes turquoise-blue with innumerable geometrical lines, diagrams and designs. When there is a fresh heavy snowfall, the whole surface becomes pure white.

The ice near the coasts bursts sometimes, and huge blocks of ice are pushed on to the shores up to 24 feet with heaps of small pebbles, big stones, sand, etc., from the bed of the Lake. Sometimes massive blocks of ice are bodily lifted and hurled from the bed of the Lake on to the shore, carrying with them small pebbles, big stones, mud, and sand. These blocks of ice melt away in spring and the pebbles, stones, sand, etc., are left in heaps or spread in beds on the shores, which conspicuously stand out different from those on the banks. When pilgrims go there in summer, they are perplexed to see the materials from the bed of the Lake on the shores at such distances from the edges.

CHAPTER III

MELTING OF MANASAROVAR

The breaking of ice and its melting into clear blue waters is even a more interesting and awe-inspiring sight than the freezing of the Lake. A month before thawing sets in along the west and south coasts, at the mouths of the Ding tso and the Tag, ice melts and forms a fine and picturesque blue border, 100 yards to half a mile in breadth, to the milk-white garment of the Lake. Here and there are seen pairs of graceful swans majestically sailing on the perfectly smooth surface of that blue border setting up small ripples on either side of their course. Especially in the mornings they do not play in the waters or engage themselves in 'belly-filling' but sail calmly towards the sun with half-closed eyes in a meditative mood and at the same time enjoying a good sun-bath. One such sight is a hundred times more effective, impressive, and sufficient to put one into a meditative mood than a series of artificial sermons or got-up speeches from a pulpit. So it is that our ancestors and *Rishis* used to keep themselves in touch with Mother Nature to have a glimpse of the Grand Architect. Small sheets and pieces of ice are also seen drifting in the blue borders, with a flying couple of swans resting on them now and then. About 11 days before breaking, the disturbance in the Lake becomes most intense between 6 and 10 A.M. and terrible sounds, rumblings, groanings, crashes resembling the roars of lions and tigers, trumpets of elephants, blowing up of mountains with dynamites, and booming of cannon are heard. One can hear notes of all sorts of musical instruments and cries of all animals. The agitation and the sounds are, in all probability, due to the ice tearing itself off and breaking asunder both in the fissures, and the minor lines of cleavage, for, the chasms in the main fissures are seen 50 to 80 feet broad with blue waters. The white ice-garment on the Holy Lake presents a fine and beautiful spectacle like a huge Bengali *sari* with broad blue borders both at the edges and in the middle. Nine days before the breaking of the Lake, the coastward sheets of ice, ranging in length from a few yards to half a mile, get isolated from the main sheet of ice along the fissures and the other lines of cleavage and are drifted by winds mostly to the western, southern, and parts of the eastern shores, to be stranded there in part, depending upon the way and velocity with which they approach the banks. The remaining portions of the sheets which still remain floating in the Lake, dash against one another and break into pieces, the smaller of which melt away in a day and the bigger remain for a few days more near the shores, sharing the fate of others. When these sheets of ice drift towards the shores in the evenings, they appear to be moving very slowly but their velocity can very well be perceived when they are partly stranded on the shores to lengths ranging from 6 to 90 feet. It is thrilling to see the lightning rapidity with which these torn pieces of ice get up on the shores with great grating noises. These are stranded on the shores either as 1 to 2 feet thick sheets or in heaps 2 to 6 feet high or in smaller heaps of smooth thin glassy sheets. It is rather curious to note that the stranded sheets of ice break up into small and big brick-like pieces, the sides of which resemble the sides of pieces of mercury sulphide.

After thus exhibiting a series of interesting and versatile transformations, the whole of the remaining Lake, all of a sudden, one night breaks into a clear beautiful and charming blue expanse to the surprise and joy of the villagers and pilgrims on the shores, the next morning, who immediately climb up to their house-tops and hail the vast expanse, extending before them even like the very sky overhead ; they show the same enthusiasm as they do when they find her frozen in winter, hoisting coloured flags, burning incense, telling prayers, and exclaiming words of praise to the gods in heavens. Tibetans believe that the Holy Manasarovar breaks on the full-moon or new-moon day or on the 10th day of the bright or dark half of the lunar month. But contrary to their traditions the Manas broke on the 12th day of the dark fortnight—*Vaisakha Krishna Dwadasi* according to North Indian almanac and *Chaitra Krishna Dwadasi* according to South Indian calendar, corresponding to May 7, in the year 1937. One forgets himself for hours together gazing at the beauty, charm, and grandeur of the oceanic Lake, teeming with pairs of graceful swans here and there merrily tossed up and down the waves. On account of the high waves dashing against one another, illusory pairs of white foamy swans make their appearance, which it is very difficult to distinguish from the real ones. When the Lake broke finally, some bigger sheets of ice remained unmelted and were drifted to the north coast which also eventually collided against one another on account of severe winds and broke into pieces and melted away within three days in the blue depths.

Two or three weeks before the Lake breaks, a peculiar change occurs in the texture and hardness of the ice. What could not have been struck and broken into smaller pieces even by means of crowbars in winter, now becomes so brittle that a blow with a stick breaks it up into small pieces. The sheets of ice that have drifted and piled up on the shores (during the week before the breaking of the Lake), when kicked, crumble down to small crystals, like those of saltpetre. When I would go out for a walk in the evenings I used to knock down several such heaps of brittle ice and amuse myself as they crumbled down into tiny crystals to melt away in a couple of days. One cannot get a solid piece of hard ice, as big as a cocoanut, from any of these heaps; but some of the huge blocks of ice that are hurled and piled up on the shores by coastal explosions during winter, cannot be moved by half a dozen strong men and exist for as many as 20 to 30 days after the breaking of the Lake.

Unlike the Manasarovar, the Rakshas Tal freezes 15 to 20 days earlier and melts again 2 to 4 weeks later. It may be mentioned in passing that this is quite the opposite of what Sven Hedin relates, namely, that " Langak-tso breaks up half a month before the Tso-mavang."* Rakshas Tal froze about 20 days earlier and broke up again nearly a month later than Manasarovar. There are many major and minor fissures and coastal eruptions in the frozen Manas, whereas the Rakshas contains only a very few. Another point of difference between the two lakes is that it takes about a week for the Rakshas Tal to freeze completely and a little more than that time to melt again completely. Sheets of ice are seen floating and drifting from side to side in the Rakshas Tal for several days even after the breaking of the lake, so much so that the Bhotia merchants going early to Tarchen Mandi (Kailas) oftentimes notice sheets of ice floating in Rakshas Tal, but not in the Manas. I noticed, and Tibetans too affirm, that the Rakshas Tal region is much colder than the Manas area and that there are greater and more massive deposits of snow all round the Rakshas. Also, the zebra-like formations of snow in well-marked stripes in the ups and downs and valleys, especially on the south and west in winter, and the islands and irregular shores with bays, gulfs, promontories, peninsulas, straits, isthmuses, rocky shores, etc., lend an additional element to the picturesqueness of the landscape around the Rakshas. Rakshas Tal would form a good model for learning geographical terms. The Manas is nearly 300 feet in depth, whereas the Rakshas is only half as deep

* 'Trans-Himalaya,' Vol. II, p. 180.

on the northern side; on the southern side it may be deeper but has not been sounded up till now. The Manas has eight monasteries and some houses on its shores and the Rakshas has only one monastery, Tsapgye,* on the north-west and the only house of the *goba* of Shungba on the west. The area of the Manas is 200 square miles and that of the Rakshas 140 square miles. The coasts of the Manas are more regular than those of her western companion. Rakshas Tal is in no way inferior to Manasarovar in physical beauty; but from the spiritual point of view the Manas is unparalleled. An interesting observation, which is a bit difficult to explain, is the temperamental difference between the two lakes though they are next-door neighbours to each other possessing areas almost of the same order of magnitude. It may be due to some local winds that the Rakshas Tal is more stormy and colder than the Manasarovar. The comparative shallowness of the Rakshas Tal may also be responsible for its shores being colder than those of the Manas, and for its freezing earlier and melting later.

Sven Hedin writes, " In winter the surface of the Tso-mavang falls 20 inches beneath the ice, which consequently is cracked and fissured, and dips from the shore; but Langak-tso sinks only one or two-thirds of an inch. This shows that it receives water constantly from the eastern lake, but only parts with a trifling quantity in winter."† Sven Hedin was on the lakes during the months of

* Also pronounced 'Chapgye.'

† 'Trans-Himalaya,' Vol. II, p. 180.

July and August but not when they froze; and so this whole information about winter must be a hearsay from some of his Tibetan guides or servants, who did certainly inform him wrongly. When the Rakshas receives water continuously from the Manas but parts with only a trifling quantity, what has become of all the 20 inches of water that has been filtered out of the Manas? If, as Sven Hedin describes, only a trifling quantity of water is filtered out of the Rakshas, the level of the water must rise. But in the same breath he says that water in the Rakshas fell down by 1 or $\frac{2}{3}$ of an inch! Could Sven Hedin expect such accurate figures from the ordinary Tibetans, who gave the figures of the levels of water in the Manas with discrepancies of several feet? So, contrary to what Sven Hedin writes, I maintain that it is not a trifling quantity of water that Rakshas Tal parts with, but almost as much quantity as it receives from the Manas, nay, even more, either by subterranean passages or otherwise, through the so-called "old bed of the Sutlej."

7. Southern View of Kailas Peak

8. Island Lachato [See page 11

9. Swans on Lachato [See page 11

10. Island Topserma [See page 12

CHAPTER IV

VEGETATION

Tibet was originally called *Bod-yul*, later on *Both*, *To-both*, *Tu-bat*, *Ti-both*, and finally *Tebet;* hence the modern name *Tibet*. Even now Tibetans call the country *Both* or *Bod* or *Chang-thang* (northern plateau), although there is a separate province called Chang-thang in Tibet. Tibet is the loftiest tableland in the world ranging from 12,000 to 16,000 feet above the sea-level, with mountains covered with eternal snows. It has an area of 814,000 square miles with a population of about 3,000,000. The region round about the Kailas and Manasarovar, extending up to the river Chhinku on the west, the source of the Indus on the north, the source of the Brahmaputra on the east, and the Indian borders on the south is called "Kailas-Manasarovar region," "Manasarovar region" or "Manasa Khanda." The region is about 130 miles from east to west and 90 to 100 miles from north to south. The population of the region may roughly be computed to be about 5,000.

In some villages of the Lake-region the grass is smooth like velvet with a carpet of brilliant tiny flowers in rose, violet, and yellow colours; at other places it is sharp and cutting like steel blades. In the upper parts of some valleys are countless designs of flowers of various hues over which botanists could very well devote some time to find out new materials for research. On one side there is a sort of sweet-scented artemisia (*davanam*) used as incense; on another side a different variety of incense fern grows in still higher regions as on the slopes of Kailas; here and there are the prickly rugged *dama* bushes (a sort of juniper), which provides the people of these parts with fire-wood, since it burns even when green and freshly cut. Excepting the *dama* bush which is hardly two to four feet high, there are no big trees. A variety of willow is specially grown here and there in the Purang valley, but no big trees which would yield timber, although poplars and other trees grow in some places of Eastern Tibet. So it is only the artist's stretch of imagination and the stroke of his brush that make Lord Shiva and Parvati sit under a huge tree at the foot of the perpetual snow-clad peak of Kailas or under a tall deodar tree on the banks of Manasarovar.

A plant called *jinbu*, the Tibetan onion, grows wildly in abundance near the hot springs of the Tag tsangpo, at Tirthapuri, Nabra, Dapa, Tuling, and at several other places in Western Tibet. *Khampas* (Tibetans domiciled in India) carry hundreds of mule-loads of dried *jinbu* plant to India, where it is used for spicing dishes. *Jeera* is a wild growth in Kardung valley and other places. In some river beds a thorny bush called *tarchima* yields a small sour fruit.

There are plenty of water-reeds in the Lake, under the surface of water. Sometimes I used to feel the smell of iodine while going on the shores. So it is just probable that the reeds might contain traces of iodine, which should interest a chemist. Here and there on the shores are swarms of a harmless and non-malarial variety of black mosquito, which may interest a research student of the Tropical School of Medicine.

Here on the shores of Manasarovar I found a wonderful drug called *thuma*. It is a marvellous specific for spermatorrhœa and an excellent aphrodisiac. *Thuma* is the root of a tiny creeper thriving at a height of 15,000 feet above the sea-level. It is not possible to collect even half a pound of it in a whole day. There is, however, an interesting way of procuring it. When the root is well ripe, wild rats collect and store it in their holes in the month of October for use in winter. The poor folk of these parts deprive the rats of their winter provisions. Just as *vidarikanda*, a big tuber used in important medical preparations by Kavirajs or Vaidyas, is eaten as food by some of the wild tribes, this root is also eaten by the poor as food for a few days. The well-to-do use it as a delicacy on special occasions like the New Year's day. The claims of this particular drug may be verified and put to test by medical men.

CHAPTER V

MINERAL RESOURCES

Almost parallel to the Ganga Chhu at a distance of about a mile on the south there is a vein of gold-deposits extending from the shores of the Manas right up to the Rakshas. They were mined some years ago but nothing is done now-a-days. During the last mining operation, it was said that there had been an outbreak of small-pox which was attributed by the Tibetans to the wrath of the presiding deity of the mines and consequently the mining was stopped by the Government. During the last mining operation it was also said that one gold nugget as big as a dog (according to another version, a dog-like nugget) was found. At the place where the nugget was found, a *chhorten* was constructed, called ' Serka-khiro ' (gold-dog). This place is at a distance of a mile south of Chiu gompa.

Some 20 days' march northwards from the shores of the Manas leads one to the extensive and rich gold-fields at Thokjalung, Munakthok, Rungmar and several other places, where they are being worked by the most primitive methods, scarcely worth the name of mining. Twenty years ago Tibetan gold was sold at the rate of Rs. 10 per tola at Lhasa, according to the account given by the

Governor of Taklakot. It is the mining experts and the enterprising capitalists that can ascertain and find ways and means to exploit these vast gold-fields on up-to-date scientific methods and on a commercial basis and can explore some more virgin gold-fields, borax-fields, and other mineral wealth. Silver, copper, iron, coal, mercury and *shilajit* are also obtained in Eastern Tibet.

Lake Tseti tso, three miles north of Gussul gompa, by the side of Manasarovar, has large deposits of borax and soda both on the shores and on the islands in it. The Tibetan Government has now stopped the working of borax at that place due to the superstitious belief that the mining deity became enraged. But some of the white deposits are carried by the people in the surroundings and used for washing hands and clothes. There are very big borax-fields at Langmar (about 140 miles from the Manas) in Western Tibet and at several other places, where in the year 1928 it was sold at the rate of 20 to 40 pounds per rupee or as much as a big goat could carry.

Tibet supplies thousands of maunds of salt from her salt lakes to a greater part of the Himalayan regions of India.

There are red- and white-wash materials on the east and the best pottery clay on the south-east of Manasarovar. There are iron and titanium sands called *chema-nenga* on the east coast and smooth pebbles on the west coast. In some other corners there are flat slabs and rounded stones used for inscribing the *mani-mantra*. Here is a volcanic rock or hill, there are alabaster-like slabs or old granite boulders, and in a third corner are some strata and fossils which may be of some importance to a geologist.

There are three hot springs on the Ganga Chhu about two furlongs from Manasarovar down the Chiu hill. One spring is on the left bank (with a *kund* to take a bath in), one on the right bank, and one boiling spring on a small rock in the middle of the Ganga Chhu. There are some in the bed of the Manasarovar, especially $\frac{3}{4}$ of a mile south of the beginning of the Ganga Chhu. About 3 or 4 miles from the shores of the Manas up on the left bank of the Tag tsangpo there are several hot springs at Tagpotong varying in range from lukewarm to boiling temperature spread over a large area, out of which a regular stream of hot water flows into the Tag. Opposite these springs on the right bank of the Tag are some caves called Chhu-phuk, where a few monks live in winter. Just near the caves there are some *chhortens* and *mani*-walls and the foundation of an old ruined monastery, said to be of Guru Padmasambhava and pulled down by the Gurkha invaders. Some shepherds of Nonokur camp here in early spring and autumn for a couple of months in each season. Near the caves and a mile down at Ambu-phuk there are some more hot springs. About $\frac{3}{4}$ of a mile up Tagpotong on the left bank of the Tag are hot springs and some boiling and bubbling geysers. This place is called Tomo-mopo. About 44 miles N.W. of Manasarovar is Tirthapuri where there are some more thermal springs, near which the demon Bhasmasura is said to have been burnt to ashes. There are large deposits of calcium carbonate and other calcium compounds all around the hot springs, which change their positions now and then and sometimes disappear altogether. There are a few more hot springs on the Sutlej at Khyunglung, a day's march down Tirthapuri. It is interesting to note that, like the beads on a string, there is a series of hot springs on the Tag at Tomomopo Tagpotong, Chhu-phuk and Anbu-phuk, in the bed of Manasarovar, in the Ganga Chhu, at Tirthapuri, and at Khyunglung.

CHAPTER VI

The People

The people both men and women in general are strong, sturdy, and hardworking; they are primitive and dirty in habits and customs, though lamas and officials are highly cultured and polite. It is only the Purang valley that is fairly well populated with fixed abodes. These abodes are flat-roofed and are often in two stories built of big sun-dried bricks and the little timber that they get from the Indian borders. The roofing is made of light timber and bushes over which mud is spread. The comparative sparseness of houses in the Kailas-Manas region is due to the fact that transit of timber to these inaccessible regions, negotiating difficult passes on yaks and ponies, is highly expensive. Sometimes even two or three houses go to make a village. Their monasteries are built similarly but on a larger scale.

About half the population of the region subsists on cattle-breeding, especially the yak, sheep and goat. They live in tents made of yak-hair, and wander from valley to valley grazing their cattle.

A part of the population of Purang also lives in caves in the hills which are made into regular houses by construction of walls and gates in the front sides. Some of the caves are even two or three-storied. Such houses are found mostly in Gukung near Taklakot, and in the villages Garu, Doh, Ringung, Dungmar, Kardung, etc. Gukung is a typical cave-village situated on the right bank of the Karnali about half a mile from Taklakot Mandi. There is a gompa also in a three-storied cave-dwelling. On the southern side of Manasarovar, situated in the uppermost part of the Namreldi valley are some caves, where the people of southern shores of the Manas took refuge in severe cold, when the brave Kashmiri General, Zoravar Singh, invaded the Manas region (in 1841?).

The staple food of the people is meat (fresh, dry, cooked, or roasted), roasted barley powder (*tsampa* or *sattu*), and large quantities of dairy products. In the morning and evening they take *thukpa*, a semi-liquid dish, that is prepared by boiling *tsampa* and meat in water, with salt added to it. The people of the Purang valley eat rice and bread also, which are supplied in large quantities from Nepal and Indian borders. They use Chinese tea in large quantities. Tea is boiled for a long time, salt and butter are added, and churned thoroughly. According to their means they drink 50 to 150 cups of tea during the day and night till they retire to bed. They take *tsampa* made into a thick paste, by mixing it with tea. *Chhang*, a light beer made from barley, is their national beverage, in which men, women, children, and monks indulge, more often on festive occasions. Tea and *chhang* are taken either in small wooden cups silvered or otherwise, in China cups or China-made stone cups by the rich, which are kept on silver stands with silver lids.

The whole region being at a height of 12,000 feet above the sea-level, it is very cold; and so Tibetans wear long double-breasted woollen gowns with a *kamarband* or waist-tier. They wear woollen shoes, called *lham*, coming almost up to the knees, which they need not remove even while entering the *Sanctum Sanctorum* of the temples in the monasteries. In winter they wear coats, trousers, and caps made of sheep or lamb-skins. When it is hot, they remove one or both hands off the coat, thereby exposing the shoulders. Women wear almost the same kind of dress as men, with the addition of a horizontally striped woollen piece in the front, from waist down to the toes, and a tanned goat-skin on the back with fur outside. Men freely use English felt hats which are brought from Calcutta and other places and sold in their marts. Rich people, officers, and lamas wear costly dresses and silks.

Polyandry is common, most probably an economic adjustment to prevent the increase of population, where struggle for existence is very hard. So when the elder brother in a family marries a wife, she thereby automatically becomes the wife of all the brothtrs and all of them live together peacefully. The wife is held in common, though the younger brothers are servants to the elder. As a result the Tibetans to-day have only as many houses and families as they had centuries ago. Monks and nuns shave their heads and wear a sort of violet-red gowns, whereas householders both men and women plait their hair. Women dress their hair in several plaits. They enjoy full social liberty. As a mark of respect or salutation Tibetans bend a little, put their tongues out and say *khamjam-bho* or simply *khamjam* or *joo*. Monks and nuns generally live freely but cannot marry legally, though sometimes nuns are seen with babes in their arms. Since monks and nuns are initiated into the order when they have absolutely no idea of the life they are to lead, it is no wonder if they do not have a high standard of morality. It is the system rather than the individuals, which is at fault. They take to all callings in life—of Gurus, high-priests, corpse-cutters, officials high and low, traders, shepherds, servants, cooks, coolies, pony-drivers, shoe-makers, smiths, cultivators, and so forth from the highest to the lowest rank—Dalai Lama to an ordinary cooly.

The manner in which the higher order of monks give their blessings, varies according to the status and social position of the blessed. The monk brings his head near the head of the other and gently touches it if he is also a high monk, or places both his hands on the heads of those he loves most, or to whom he wants to show a greater favour. In other cases he blesses the other with one hand, two fingers, or only with one finger. The last mode of blessing is by touching the head with a coloured piece of cloth tied to a short stick. The principle underlying all these is that there should be some contact of the blesser and the blessed in order to pass some power of efficacy to the latter from the former, besides invoking the usual blessings.

Tibetans have a peculiar way of killing sheep for meat. They suffocate the animal to death by tying the mouth and nostrils tightly with a rope, for it is enjoined in their religious texts that the blood of a living animal should not be spilt.

The dead bodies of well-to-do monks are cremated while those of poor monks and householders are hacked to pieces and thrown to vultures or cast into a river if there is one near by. Both birth and death ceremonies are many and complicated, varying with individual means, and are much akin to those of the Hindus. When the dead body is cremated, the ashes are mixed with clay and moulded into a small pyramid which is kept in a monument known as *chhorten* corresponding to the *stupa* in India.

Buddhism was first introduced into Tibet in the time of King Srongchen Sampo, who reigned between 630 and 698 A.D. It flourished for several years under the royal patronage. The religion of the Tibetans is primarily Buddhism with a queer admixture of *Tantricism* or *Saktaism* and the old *Bon Dharma* (pre-Buddhistic religion of devil-worshipping). Tibet is predominantly a priest-ridden country, and as such some Western writers call the religion of Tibet *Lamaism.* One or two children from every family are initiated into the order of monks and nuns at the age of two or three. Nearly one-third or one-fourth of the population consists of monks and nuns and the standard of morality is low. The Buddhism prevalent in Tibet is of the Mahayana School.

Most of the monks are attached to the monasteries called *gompas,* solitary places. Gompas are a combination of a temple (where the images of

Buddha and other Buddhistic deities are kept and worshipped), a *math* (where monks have their board and lodging), and a *dharmashala* (where travellers and pilgrims get a lodging). The first monastery in Tibet was built between 823 and 835 A.D. at Samye on the model of Udantapuri. Bigger monasteries also serve the purpose of schools and are big educational centres. As a matter of fact, the four great Universities of Tibet are situated in the monasteries of Depung with 7,700 monks, Sera with 5,500 monks, Ganden and Tashi Lhumpo with 3,300 monks each.

Elementary education is generally given to monks in almost all the monasteries of Tibet. One has to go for higher education to some of these big Universities near Lhasa as there are no big educational centres in Western Tibet (*Ngari*). All the above-mentioned Universities or Monastic Colleges are residential. Besides religious education, grammar, literature and medicine, image-making, engraving, painting, printing, etc., are also taught. All these Universities and monasteries are maintained by big landed properties attached to them, by public charity, and also by the trading and banking business conducted by some of the monks in the monasteries. Out of the total strength of the Universities only half the number are regular students and the rest of the monks are servants, conductors, managers, tradesmen, etc. Students from different places like Rampur Bushahr State, Ladakh, Southern Russia and Siberia, and China go to these Monastic Universities for study. Almost all of them are monks.

Monks are of two orders : *lamas* or superior order of monks and *dabas* or ordinary monks. It is after studying both religious and ritual texts for several years that one is made a lama. There are different orders—high, middle, and low—amongst lamas also. All monks including lamas indulge in drinking and meat-eating. Tibetans in general have no religious bigotry though they are very superstitious and their monasteries can be visited by people of any religion. All the monasteries of Western Tibet were built after the ninth century A.D.

The two great Tibetan works in the shelves of a Tibetan library are *Kanjur* (or *Kangyur*—translation of Lord Buddha's actual utterances) in 108 volumes and *Tanjur* (or *Tangyur*—translation of *Shastras*) in about 235 volumes. These works comprise different Schools of Philosophy, *Kavyas*, Grammar, Astrology, Astronomy, *Devata Sadhana*, *Tantras* and *Mantras* besides the commentaries on several books of *Kanjur* and Tibetan translations of the Chinese renderings of some original Sanskrit works. *Tanjur* also contains the translations of several other Sanskrit works, whose originals were for ever lost in the bonfires of the various ruthless Muhammadan invaders and kings. It also contains the lost works of the great astronomer Aryadeva, Dingnaga, Dharmarakshita, Chandrakirti, Shantirakshita and Kamalasila, the unknown works of Lokananda *Natak*, Vadanyaya *tika* of the great grammarian Chandragoumi, and also several lost works of Aswaghosh, Matichitra, Haribhadra, Aryasura, and others and some works of Kalidasa, Dandi, Harshavardhana, and other great poets.

The medical works of Ashtanga Hridaya of Nagarjuna, Shilihotra and others with commentaries and glossaries and the translations of some Hindi books and also of some of the letters of Yogishawar Jagadratna to Kanishka, the letters of Dipankara Sreejnana to Raja Nayapala (of Pala Dynasty) are in the volumes of *Tanjur*. Besides these two voluminous collections of works the lives of Nagarjuna, Aryadeva, Asanga, Vasubandhu, Shantarakshita, Chandrakirti, Dharmakirti, Chandragoumi, Kamalasila, Shila, Deepankara Sreejnana and other Indian Buddhist Pandits are also written in Tibetan language.

When Buddhism was introduced into Tibet in the time of King Srongchen about the year 641 A.D., at his order his minister Thonmi invented an alphabet on the model of the characters of the Kashmiri Sharada alphabet then current, in order to put the Tibetan translations of Pali and Sanskrit Buddhist and other works into writing. Necessary modifications have been made, so as to include the sounds peculiar to the Tibetan language. Thonmi wrote the first grammar of the Tibetan language. Before his time writing was unknown in Tibet.

In the beginning of the fourteenth century Rinchhen Grub collected all the translations of Buddha's works under the title *Kanjur* and all the *Shastras* under the title *Tanjur*. It was in the year 1728 (?) that the *Kanjur* and the *Tanjur* were printed for the first time during the régime of the seventh Dalai Lama. But according to another version it was in the middle of the seventeenth century, the régime of the fifth Dalai Lama, that these works were printed. Whole pages of books are engraved on wooden blocks and printed. Books are printed on country-made paper of three qualities—common, superior and superfine. Books produced in the last edition have thick strong paper and the letters are printed in gold. If the two works of *Kanjur* and *Tanjur* were to be re-translated into Sanskrit, it would come to about 20 lakhs of *slokas*.

About the year 1027 A.D., Pandit Somnath of Kashmir translated the " Kala Chakra Jyotisha " into Tibetan and introduced the Brihaspati cycle of sixty years called *Prabhava*, etc. (*Rabyung* in Tibetan). This cycle of sixty years is divided into five sub-cycles of twelve years each. At the beginning of each of these sub-cycles (*i.e.*, once in twelve years) a big fair is held near Kailas at Sershung. The Kumbha mela of India, which recurs once in 12 years, has nothing to do with this fair, as confounded by several people. *Margasirsha Sukla Pratipada* (which fell on December 14 in 1936) is observed as New Year's day on the southern shores of Manasarovar, as in the days of the *Mahabharata*, and this may be of interest to the Indian astronomer. Tibetans of that region say that the sun begins his northward journey from that day. *Pushya Sukla Pratipada* (which fell on January 13 in 1937) is observed as New Year's day on the eastern side of the Manas (Horba) and *Magha Sukla Pratipada* (which fell on February 12 in 1937) is the official New Year's day throughout Tibet. Special *pujas* and services are conducted in the monasteries on the New Year's day, and feastings and merry-making take place for 10 to 15 days, in which monks and

1. Holy Mount Kailas.
2. Tijung.
3. Tsering Chenga.
4. Nyanri Peak.
5. Ponri Peak.
6. Gurla Mandhata.
7. Thuki Zingboo.
8. Tso Kapala.
9. Kurkyal Chhungo.
10. Holy Lake Manasarovar.
11. Rakshas Tal or Ravan Hrad.
12. Lachato.
13. Topserma.
14. Lha Chhu.
15. Tarchen Chhu.
16. Zhong Chhu.
17. Ganga Chhu.
18. Samo Tsangpo.
19. Tag Tsangpo.
20. Nimapendi.
21. Tarchen.
22. Parkha.
23. Nyanri Gompa.
24. Zunthulphuk Gompa.
25. Gengta Gompa.
26. Silung Gompa.
27. Gossul Gompa.
28. Chiu Gompa.
29. Cherkip Gompa.
30. Langpona Gompa.
31. Ponri Gompa.
32. Seralung Gompa.
33. Yerngo Gompa.
34. Thugolho Gompa (Thokar).
35. Tsapgye Gompa.
36. Tarchen Chhak-chhal-gang.
37. Tarbohchhe (flag-staff).
38. Chhorten Kangnyi.
39. Shapje (footprint).
40. Hanumanjoo.
41. Serdung Chuksum.
42. Dolma La.
43. Shapje-dakthok.
44. Tarko La or Sera La.
    Chak-chhal-gang.

(To face the Plate facing p. 48)

11. Central part of Kailas-Manasarovar region, from a Tibetan painting | *See pages 5, 6, 13*

12. The Governor of Taklakot and his Secretary [*See page 65*

householders, both men and women, freely participate.

The third day of the bright half of a lunar month, dedicated to Padmasambhava or Guru Rinpochhe, the eighth day dedicated to *Devi*, the full-moon day dedicated to Lord Buddha, and the new-moon day, are the days in each lunar month, on which special *pujas* are performed in the monasteries, besides some other days which differ from place to place. *Damarus*, conchs, drums, cymbals, bells, clarinets, flutes, pipes of human bones, and some other musical instruments, *dorje* (thunderbolt), human skulls, several cups of water and barley, incense, butter-lamps, *chhang*, *tsampa*, meat, butter, cakes, and several other things are used in the worship of deities in the monasteries. A loosely woven gauze-like white linen called *khatak*, about 9 inches broad and 3 feet long, is used as a garland for the deities in the image-halls. It is also offered to the officials and monks before having an interview with them. Now and then big *yantras* are drawn and images of *tsampa* and butter in several colours are made of different deities and elaborate *pujas* are conducted from 3 to 30 days, mostly according to *tantric* rites. On the last day of the worship a big *havan* is performed. Several water-colour paintings called *thankas* or banner paintings are hung in the image halls, library halls and other rooms. The paintings represent deities, lamas, scenes, *yantras*, etc., and have silk borders and veils over them to protect them from being damaged. Tibet owes a great deal to India for the development of her religion, civilization, learning, painting and other arts.

Om-ma-ni-pad-me-hum is the most popular and sacred *mantra* of the Tibetans, which is ever on the lips of all men, women, children, monks, and householders. They always repeat this *mantra*—whether sitting, walking or travelling. Even the ordinary Tibetan repeats this *mantra* for a greater number of times than a most orthodox Brahmin does his *Gayatri Japa* in India. The meaning of this formula is " The Jewel of *Om* in the Heart-Lotus." The word *hri* is also added to it very often. As in *Tantric* schools, Tibetans assign certain colours to each letter of the *mantra* and they believe that the utterance of this six-syllabled formula extinguishes re-birth in the six worlds and secures *Nirvana*. The colours of the letters are white, blue, yellow, green, red, and black respectively. *Hri* is also said to be white. The *mani-mantra* is said to be an invocation of the Bodhisattva Avalokiteswara.

The *mani-mantra* is inscribed, embossed or painted on walls, rocks, stones, slabs, caves, monasteries, on horns, bones, flags—on everything. The *mantra* is engraved on round stones or slabs which are kept on walls at the entrance of villages, on the tops of passes at camping grounds, on the way to holy places and monasteries, at spots wherefrom some holy place is seen, and at every important place. The *mantra* is written several times on slips of paper which are kept in a small brass, copper or silver cylinder with a handle. The prayer wheel, cylinder or mill (*korlo*) is turned round and round in the clock-wise direction by all monks, beggars, men and women. One round of the wheel is believed to be productive of as much virtue as the repetition of the *mantra* as many times as it is written on the slips in the cylinder. Several such *mani*-cylinders of different sizes are set up at the gates of and inside the monasteries, and are revolved by the pilgrims when they visit them. I saw some such big *mani*-cylinders in Ladakh, driven by water-power, like *pan-chakkis* (water-mills). They contain slips of paper, on which the *mani-mantra* is written a lakh, a million or even ten million times.

Just above the Taklakot Mandi, situated on the top of a hill, overlooking the Mandi and the neighbouring villages and the Karnali with its feeders, is the famous Similing gompa, the biggest monastery of this region. It has about 8 branch monasteries at Siddikhar, on Manasarovar and at other places. Including the branches it has about 250 monks of whom 6 are *lamas* and the rest *dabas*. There is a regular school for the junior monks of the monastery. Some of the village boys also are educated here. In the central image-hall of the monastery there is a big gilded image of Lord Buddha, about 6 feet high, seated on a high pedestal, with butter-lamps kept burning in the front. Once in a year there are held general feasts, merry-making, and devil-dances by the monks, lasting for a week or two. In the devil-dance, they wear long gowns and a variety of masks of devils and demons of queer shapes. The devil-dance of Similing monastery is called *Torgyak*, that of Khochar gompa *Namdong*, and that of Siddikhar monastery *Tsege*. When any distinguished person visits a monastery, the monks receive him to the accompaniment of the musical instruments of the gompa. There are some hundreds of Tibetan books in the shelves of the library rooms of the monastery, including the two voluminous works of *Kanjur* and *Tanjur*.

Situated on the left bank of the river Karnali is the famous Khochar or Khocharnath gompa, at a distance of about 12 miles south-east of Taklakot Mandi. Khochar is one of the most interesting monasteries in Western Tibet. In the image-hall there are three beautiful images of three of the most important Bodhisattvas, made of *ashta dhatus* (eight metals), standing on a beautifully designed pedestal or a bracket about 5 feet high. The middle image *Jambyang* (Manjushree) is about 8 feet high with four hands, of which two are golden and two of silver. On its right is the idol of *Chenresi* (Avalokiteswara) 7 feet high, and on the left is the idol of *Chhanadorje* (Vajrapani) 7 feet high and of blue complexion. These three images are erroneously described as, and believed by, many credulous people to be those of Rama, Lakshmana and Seeta. It is interesting to note that all the three images are of male deities! Tibetans believe that these images along with the pedestal (*simhasana*) on which they are set up have sprung out of the boulder on which they stand through some divine origin and not made by any human hand. The images and the pedestal are of South Indian pattern and were prepared by the Nepalese sculptors. There are several cups containing water, and butter-lamps made of gold and silver, artistically arranged in front of the images. There are six big and fierce-looking images each about 8 feet high at the entrance gate of the monastery. These images are probably of *lokapalas*. I understand that there are about 50 *dabas* with a *Tulku lama* in the monastery. There is a big hall in the second building of the monastery, where a type of devil-dance called *Namdong* and annual feasts are held. In the hall are hung a stuffed wild yak and an Indian tiger on one side. There are also the images of *Chamba** (Maitreya), Mahakala and Mahakali, Sange-Pavo-Rapdun,† and Yum-Chhamo-Chhok-Chu-Sange,‡ placed in different rooms. There is a big *mani*-cylinder 10 feet high and 5 feet in diameter.

Several sensational articles are freely published both in the East and in the West about the *Mahatmas* and *Siddhas*§ in this little seen and less studied part of the world, namely Tibet. Most of the stories gaining currency here are mere exaggerations or misrepresentations and are more of the nature of stunts than anything else. I may mention here that I visited altogether about 50 monasteries (*i.e.*, almost all the monasteries of Western Tibet and most of them in Ladakh) and met not less than 1,500 monks, both *lamas* and *dabas*. But never did I come across any great *Siddha* or a *Yogi* worth mentioning in the whole of Western Tibet. There are no doubt several *lamas* who are learned in their scriptures and well-versed in the external *Tantric*

* Also pronounced 'Champa.'

† Buddha-hero-seven or Seven Buddhas. These seven idols are not of those of *Saptarshis*—Agastya, etc., but of the seven Buddhas—Kashyapa Buddha, Maitreya Buddha, Goutama Buddha, etc.

‡ Mother-great-directions-ten-Buddhas. These eleven idols are of Great Mother and of Ten Buddhas, but not of Eleven *Rudras* as believed and described by the Hindu pilgrims.

§ One who has attained high psychic and supernatural powers.

rites and incantation-performances, which are elaborately conducted for days together. People in general are very superstitious, religious-minded, devotional, and mystic in temperament. I did not meet any really spiritually advanced *lamas* or *yogis* nor any monk 90 or 100 years old, though some people claim to have seen sages like Vyasa and Aswatthama and other monks thousands of years old with corporeal bodies. Personally I would neither accept such credulous statements nor would force others to disbelieve them but would prefer to leave the matter to individual judgment and discrimination.

This is not to say, however, that really great *Mahatmas* or saints and *Yogis* do not exist; nor should this statement be misconstrued to mean that I am sceptical about the reality of the existence of these advanced souls, as I consider my own Revered Master Dr. Swami Jnanananda to be one such adept, who, though he failed in the Matriculation Examination, could give out through his intuitional knowledge (knowledge revealed in higher spiritual states) certain equations in the Spectroscopy of X-Radiations* which turned out to be more precise than the existing equations of Sir William Bragg. It took about three years of continuous and laborious work for the equations to be verified experimentally in the Charles University of Prague. The simple fact remains that really spiritually advanced yogis or lamas are as rare a phenomenon here as

* One can refer to 'New and Precise Methods in the Spectroscopy of X-Radiations' by Dr. Swami Jnanananda, M.M.P.S., F.R.S.S., Prague.

anywhere else. I was, however, informed by the Governor of Purang Taklakot, of monks being immured for some years, and in a few cases for life, in Eastern Tibet. But this practice is in the nature of mortification or miracle rather than a symbol of high spiritual attainment. During my several visits to Tibet I had the good fortune of coming across a lama from Lhasa (aged about 50) in the year 1936 and of having the rare privilege of attending some *Tantric* rites (which non-Tibetans are not allowed to attend) he conducted in the Similing monastery of Taklakot for three days continuously. He was a good *Sadhaka* and a *Tantric*. I also met a young *Tulku lama* (incarnation monk) aged 16, in Ponri gompa* in the year 1928, who, I felt was an elevated soul. These are the only notables whom I happened to meet. It is really regrettable to find some people fabricating curious and funny stories which are utterly false, to trade upon the credulity of the innocent and religiously minded folk. There is no doubt, however, that the surroundings of the Holy Kailas and Manasarovar are highly charged with spiritual vibrations of a supreme order, which make one exhilarated and elevated.

There are many more things of interest, to some of which only it is possible here to make a mere passing reference. I have often been asked about the existence of golden lotuses, pearls and the traditional *Rajahansas* or royal swans in Manasarovar and about the *Mahatmas* and Tibetan mystics around Kailas and Manasarovar. In this connection I may

* The fifth monastery of Manasarovar.

say without any fear of contradiction that the first two are totally mythological. As regards the third, namely swans, it may be noted that there are chiefly three distinct species of water-birds in these regions. The first, called *ngangba* in Tibetan, which to my mind corresponds to the traditional swan, is white or pale-ash in colour. Local people assert it to be a pure vegetarian that lives merely on moss, grass and water-reeds. It does not touch fish, oysters or snails. This is considered holy and the Tibetans do not kill it even for their table although they are not as scrupulous about the eggs, which are freely consumed. This species of the bird exists on the smaller islet Lachato in the Rakshas Tal even more abundantly than in the Manas, the reason probably being that except for a short period in winter, neither men nor wolves can reach there and lay hold on them or their eggs. These swans daily go to the so-called " old bed of the Sutlej " in winter, to eat grass and moss. The servants of Kardung *goba* go to the island in the first week of April for collecting eggs. They go there and return within two weeks, for, after that time the island is cut off from the mainland by the breaking of ice near the shores. It is said that 2 to 4 thousand eggs are collected in those two weeks. These eggs are 3 to 4 times the size of a normal hen's eggs. Swans are found in large numbers in the Manas near Thugolho, Yushup tso, Gussul, Tseti tso, Chiu gompa, Ganga Chhu, Kurkyal Chhungo, Ding tso, and at the mouths of the Samo and the Tag. These swans lay their eggs under small sand-hills. In late spring one can see these birds breasting the waves in pairs, keeping a number of young ones in their midst. They swim in the water producing diverging ripples in the calm Lake.

The second variety of birds, called *ngaru-sirchung*, are like ducks and almond brown in complexion. The third variety, called *chakarma*, are snow-white in colour except at the head, tail, and part of the wings, which are black. They feed freely and mostly on fish, etc., and resemble partly the swan and partly the stork. Herons are also seen near Ding tso, Kurkyal Chhungo and in the so-called "old bed of the Sutlej." I am of opinion that swan, goose, wild goose, duck, wild duck, gull, etc., are all of the same family or genus and that the swan is not a mere mythological creation as some believe it to be, since we see the black variety with graceful necks in Australia and the white one in India. Recently I read in some scientific magazine that "swans had been known to attain their second century." It is for the ornithologist to give a final verdict.

Smooth pebbles of various shapes and colours are picked up from the west coast; a sort of violet sand named *chema-nenga*, which is a mixture of five sands of red, black, yellow, white, and green colours, is picked up from the east coast, where it is found in thin layers, only for a distance of about three miles, and the water of the Lake is taken in corked bottles or vessels by pilgrims as *prasads* or mementos of the Holy Manasarovar. This sand of Manasarovar is found on chemical examination to contain emery, iron, and titanium, the last two of which are used in the manufacture of steel. A variety of light-scented artemisia plant (*davanam*) is also taken as the incense of Manasarovar, which can be purchased from the monasteries. Another variety of scented fern, called *Kangri po* or Kailas incense, grows around Kailas at a height of over 16,000 feet above the sea-level. This fern is dried and used as an incense.

Fishes, big and small, abound in the Lake, which, when beaten by high dashing waves, die and are drifted to the shore and stranded. These dead fish are picked up, dried in the sun and are taken by the pilgrims as *prasad* of the Holy Lake. They are preserved carefully, or are used as incense, which is said to have the efficacy of dispelling evil spirits, of effacing the evil influence of planets and of curing various cattle diseases. Dried fish are sold by the monks in the monasteries. But nobody kills a fish in the Lake.

CHAPTER VII

AGRICULTURE AND ECONOMIC LIFE

The whole valley consisting of about 30 villages including Taklakot is called Purang valley and is cultivated. Excepting the villages in the Purang valley the whole of Kailas-Manasarovar region is a barren tract. Barley and pea are grown in sufficient quantities in the valley. The fields are cultivated by water from the hill-streams distributed into small nice channels. The channels are bordered by green grass and present a pleasing appearance in the bleak and barren country. Ploughing is done by *jhabbus* (cross breed of Indian cow and Tibetan bull the yak) or ponies since yak is not good for ploughing though useful for carrying heavy loads. It is said that agriculture was introduced into Tibet in the beginning of the Christian era during the reign of Byakhri. King Srongchen Sampo (630-698) introduced the earthen pot, water-mill and hand-loom. There are water-mills (*pan-chakkis*) for grinding barley, in some of the villages of the valley wherever there are hill-streams or channels taken out of them.

Yak, horse, a variety of snow-leopard, wolf, ibex, goat, hare, and a variety of marmot or a big monkey-like rat are the chief wild animals of the Manas region and Tibet in general. The marmots remain in hibernation in their holes under several feet of snow for 4 or 5 months in winter. It is perhaps by observing these marmots and frogs that yogis evolved *Khechari Mudra*, in which they remain for days together in *Samadhi* (trance) without any signs of external growth or decay. The fat and skins of these marmots are considered very effective for rheumatism, which is very common in those cold regions. Excepting vultures, crows, pigeons, and birds of the swan family I did not notice many birds. Wild yaks live in herds at heights above 16,000 feet as at the source of Brahmaputra and the Dunglung valley on the north-west of Kailas. These are ferocious animals and are hunted by Tibetans for meat. Wild horses, called *kiyangs*, roam in large herds throughout Tibet on the table-lands where pasture is in abundance; but they are neither tamed nor hunted. Musk is collected in large quantities from the musk-deer in Eastern Tibet and exported to China. The chief domestic animals are yak (Tibetan hairy bull), *jhabbu*, horse, mule, ass, sheep, and goat. There goes a Bhotia saying that sheep, goats and yaks are the chief crop and wealth of Tibetans. Occasionally once in 7 or 8 years, when the snowfall is heavy, the pasture-lands are buried under snow for days together, and hundreds of animals from the herds have no alternative but to die of starvation and severe cold, as all domestic animals including dogs, sheep, horses, yaks, etc., are always kept in open compounds without roofs, even in the severest winters.

The yak is a great beast of burden and carries heavy loads even on bad roads and higher altitudes;

but it cannot withstand the hot climate and dense air of lower altitudes nor can it be used for tilling the land. *Jhabbu* on the other hand can withstand hot climate and dense air of the lower altitudes, and the cold climate and the rarified air of higher altitudes. It is useful both for ploughing the land and for carrying loads. So the Bhotias of the Mandis in Tibet and the Tibetans of Taklakot keep a good number of *jhabbus*. Some of the yaks and *jhabbus* with nose-strings are also used for riding.

Tibet is a big wool-producing country. Thousands of maunds of wool are imported into India every year from the Manasarovar region and other parts of Tibet. All the woollen mills of northern India and Bombay get the major part of their wool supplies from Tibet. Sometimes there are indents for Tibetan wool from foreign countries. If the wool produce of Tibet is controlled and improved scientifically, Tibet will become one of the finest and biggest wool-supplying countries of the world-market, like Switzerland. Besides supplying wool, the millions of sheep are the chief means of conveyance in and across the Himalayas for carrying enormous quantities of wool, salt, and borax from Tibet to India ; and grains and miscellaneous goods from India to Tibet. Though Tibet is purely a Buddhist country by religion, half the food of a Tibetan consists of mutton. There is a Bhotia saying that sheep are the goods trains, ponies and mules mail trains. It is a pleasant sight to watch hundreds of sheep moving slowly with double panniers of salt or grains on their backs, going along the trails up and down the mighty Himalayan ranges, plodding their weary way, picking up every now and then hurriedly a blade of grass here and a mouthful there. The approach of these laden sheep is often announced by the rising of clouds of dust and the peculiar whistlings of the Bhotia drivers and by the voice of the little bells tied to the necks of some of the animals, the tinkling of which sounds and resounds along the forest roads. Generally the Tibetan sheep are not unloaded till they reach the destination, for it is a very tedious business to load these restive and turbulent creatures.

Cheese (called *chhura* in Tibetan), butter, milk, and other dairy products of the Singi Khambab locality are considered the best in the whole of Tibet. There are thousands of *yaks* and *demas* (Tibetan bulls and cows) and millions of sheep and goats in Tibet. Good dairy farms may be started on up-to-date scientific lines with great profit and advantage, as Tibet is mainly a pastoral country where the chief occupation of the people is cattle-breeding. Crude Tibetan cheese can be had at the rate of two annas per pound and butter at the rate of 2 to 3 pounds per rupee. Butter is very badly stored in raw sheep-skins. Thousands and thousands of sheep—rather solid and compact masses of sheep, spread over miles and miles together, are seen moving and grazing on the shores and slopes of Manasarovar.

There are several Mandis or marts of Bhotia* merchants in Western Tibet, most of which are

* Indian borderland of North Almora, North Garhwal, North Tehri, etc., is called *Bhot*. People of Bhot are called Bhotias. Bhot and Bhotias should not be confused with Bhutan State or the Bhutanese. Tibetans are called Hunias by the Bhotias.

situated in the Kailas-Manas region. These Mandis are held for periods ranging from a fortnight to five months. Gyanima Mandi (also known as Kharko) of Johar Bhotias, Chhakra Mandi (also known as Gyanima Chhakra) of Darma Bhotias, Taklakot Mandi (also known as Pilithanka) of Chaudans and Byans Bhotias, Nabra Mandi of Niti Bhotias, and Gukung Mandi of the Nepalese are the biggest. Tarchen (Kailas), and Thokar (Thugolho-Manasarovar), and Gartok Mandis come next in order, of which the first two are big wool-shearing centres. Puling, Tuling, Lama Chhorten, and Dayul Chhongra Mandis are smaller. Gyanima is the biggest of the Mandis in Western Tibet where a transaction of about 25 lakhs of rupees is done annually. In almost all these Mandis wool, coarse Tibetan blankets, sheep, ponies, mules, borax, salt, hides, etc., are either sold for cash or exchanged for the commodities of the Indian merchants, namely, piece-goods, *gur* (jaggery), barley, wheat, rice, utensils, Chinese tea, etc. All the commodities which are available in Indian markets are also procurable here.

There are freebooters of nomadic tribes everywhere in Tibet. They are shepherds wandering from place to place with their sheep, ponies, yaks, kith and kin, and some of them move towards Kailas and Manasarovar also for trade and pilgrimage between May and October. Since no restriction is imposed by the Tibetan Government as regards possessing arms, these nomads carry swords, daggers, old Tibetan matchlock guns, Russian and German pistols, revolvers and rifles with plenty of gunpowder and cartridges. When they come across any unarmed traders or pilgrims, they loot them and make good their escape into some ravines or to some distant places. The Tibetan Government makes no arrangement to arrest them.

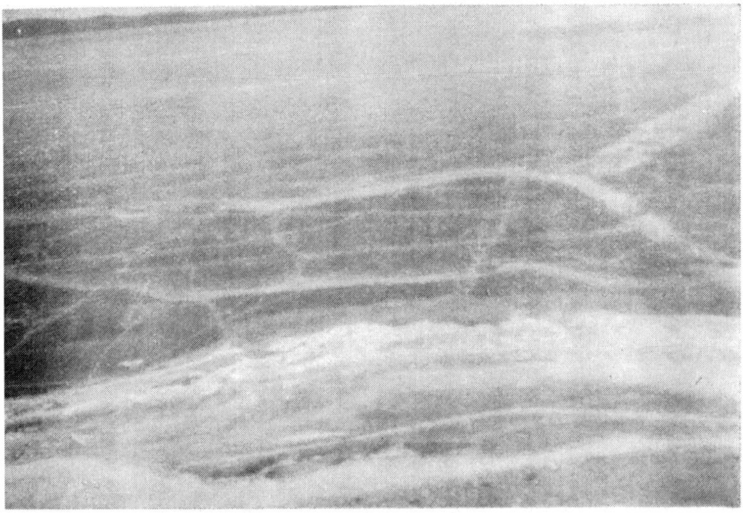

13. Fissures in frozen Manasarovar [*See page 20*

14. Unfissured Ice of Rakshas Tal, seen from Lachato Island towards Topserma [*See page 20*

15. Manasarovar frozen, with fissures and regular blocks of ice piledup into embankments due to coastal explosions [See page 21

CHAPTER VIII

Administration

The whole of Tibet is ruled by Dalai Lama (the High Monk, said to be the incarnation of the Bodhisattva Avalokiteswara) and the council of native officers (both monks and householders) acting under the advice of the Chinese Resident. It is said that the first Dalai Lama was born in 1391 A.D. and the thirteenth died in December, 1933. Others say that this system of "incarnation Dalai Lama" came into existence in 1284. The capital is at Lhasa (11,900 feet) with a population of about 40,000, about one-half of which consists of monks and nuns.

Western Tibet, wherein are situated the Holy Kailas and Manasarovar, is governed by two *Garpons* or *Urkos* (Viceroys), one senior (*Urko-Kong*) and one junior (*Urko-Yok*). The summer capital is Gartok and the winter capital Gargunsa. Western Tibet is divided into four provinces, *viz.*, Rudok, Purang-Taklakot, Dapa, and Chhabrang, each in charge of a *Zong* or *Zongpon*. The Kailas-Manasarovar region is under the jurisdiction of Purang Zong, excepting the tract west of Chhakra Mandi. Gyanima is under the jurisdiction of Dapa Zong.

Besides these there are *Chhasus* or Tax Collectors in the marts, *Yung Chhong* or Government Trade Agents or Merchants, and *Tazams* or *Tarzams* or *Tasams* (Post-stages or conveyance offices and officers) who are readily to supply transport animals to Government officials going up and down. These *Tasams* also convey State mails between Lhasa and Gartok and other Government centres. Out of the 25 *Tasams* stationed along the Lhasa-Gartok high road three are in the Kailas-Manas region. For the last four years, regular postal stamps have been in use in Tibet for conveyance of letters and parcels from Lhasa to various Government centres.

All the abovementioned officials are appointed direct from Lhasa for a term of three years, which may be extended by one or two more terms in some cases. The administration of villages and wandering tribal camps is carried on by *Gopas* or *Gobas* (headmen) and *Magpons* (Patwaris) over groups of villages. *Gopa* and *Magpon* are hereditary posts and are held by men of the villages concerned. None of the officials is paid by the Central Government at Lhasa ; on the contrary, these officials have to pay certain fixed amounts to the Central Government, and they have to raise this sum as well as their own profit from the civil, criminal, and revenue administration of the places under their charge. Besides this income all officials have their own enormous personal trade, for which they get conveyances from the *Tasams* practically free. For simple offences the hands of the culprit are tightly bound together with a woollen rope until they bleed, clothes are stripped off, and he is awarded 40 to

300 lashes on his buttocks and back. For serious offences like dacoities the hands of the offender are cut off at the wrists and then dipped into boiling oil in order to prevent the wound from becoming septic; for more serious crimes and for political offences against the State, the accused is brutally killed by redhot iron rods being thrust into his temples and the removal of the eyes, or by being hurled down from the top of a steep rock or hill. Oftentimes both the parties in a case are heavily fined—such fines forming a great source of income to the officers.

Over one-half of the Government posts are held by monks. Women are not debarred from holding high Government positions, including even those of the Viceroys and Governors. There is practically no standing army or regular police either at the Viceregal centre at Gartok or the Governors' centres, though of late efforts are being made at Lhasa to maintain a regularly-trained police and military force. Whenever an emergency arises, men can be mustered from villages, since all Tibetans know the use of firearms.

Taklakot is the headquarters of Purang Zong and is at a distance of 11 miles from the Lipu Lekh pass, on the Indian border. On the back of a hillock are the quarters of the Governor and the famous Similing monastery. There is a prison house inside the Zong's building, where whips and handcuffs are stored. On the narrow plateau called Pilithanka, situated at the foot of the hillock, is held a big Mandi from the month of June to October. The Bhotia merchants hold the market in walled-enclosures of sun-dried bricks. Tents are set up temporarily over the walls, since, according to the treaty of 1904 made between the British and the Tibetan Government, Indians are not allowed to construct roofed houses in Tibet.

According to the same treaty three British Trade Agents are appointed—one in Eastern Tibet with headquarters at Gyantse, one at Yatung, and one in Western Tibet with headquarters at Gartok for six months, it is said, to look after the interests and grievances of the Indian traders who hold markets in Tibet every year. The British Trade Agent of Western Tibet starts from Simla in the month of May, goes to Gartok, visits the important marts, goes again to Gartok, and comes back to India by the Lipu Lekh pass and Almora in the month of November. A travelling Post Office always accompanies him wherever he goes, which delivers and despatches mails, once a week, as long as he is in Western Tibet. Garbyang (30 miles from Taklakot) and Milam are the Indian Post Offices nearest to the Kailas-Manas region.

About 3 miles north of Taklakot is the village Toyo, where there is the *samadhi* or grave of General Zoravar Singh, who invaded Tibet and annexed Ladakh to Kashmir in 1841 (?). Tibetans believe that Zoravar Singh possessed supernatural powers, and that no ordinary leaden bullet could penetrate his body; they say that he was shot in the end with a golden bullet, that he was afterwards hacked to pieces and that a monument was constructed over the hacked pieces. There still exists the monument in the form of a *chhorten*.

Tarchen, at the foot of Kailas, Nyanri and Zunthulphuk monasteries of Kailas, Cherkip gompa of the Manasarovar, the villages of Dungmar, Ringung, Doh, Khochar, Gezon near Gartok, Itse gompa, Gonphu, Gesur, Sammar, and a few other places in Western Tibet belong to the State of Bhutan. These places are governed by a Bhutanese Officer, whose headquarters are at Tarchen, where there is a big building owned by the Bhutan State.

Tanka or *tanga* is the common silver coin in use throughout Tibet. Half *tanga* called *jav* is also current. The copper coins in use in Tibet are *karma-nga* ($\frac{1}{3}$ *tanga*), *shogang* ($\frac{2}{3}$ *tanga*), and *chhegye* ($\frac{1}{2}$ *tanga*) which are exchangeable only at Lhasa. For the last few years currency notes and silver rupees have been in use at Lhasa. Indian Rupees are freely used everywhere in Tibet in transactions. Tibetans prefer the Indian Rupee to their *Tanga*. The present rate of exchange is eight *tangas* per rupee in Western Tibet and 10 or 12 at Lhasa. The Indian Rupee is called *gormo* in Tibetan. For convenience of transit, high Tibetan officials take the Indian currency notes with them when they go to Lhasa, as these are freely exchangeable there.

The possibilities of an expedition to reach the top of the Kailas (if such a venture be at all allowed by the conservative, superstitious, and suspicious Tibetans) can be investigated and surveyed from the eastern side alone, since on the remaining three sides the peak rises almost perpendicularly and since avalanches slide down it headlong.

Fine aerodromes may be constructed anywhere on Parkha Maidan north-west of Manasarovar, or on the plains on the north or south-west, or on any other plain like the one at Gyanima or Chhakra, for the landing of the aeroplanes of any enterprising " Kailas-Manasarovar Air Service Company," that may be started in future. Seaplanes can conveniently descend into the Manas or the Rakshas.

Several pilgrim and tourist parties visit Kailas and Manasarovar, from year to year. Thousands of Bhotia merchants go there annually for trade. But nobody takes interest in having a boat trip on the Manas or to the islands in the Rakshas. It would indeed be a fine thing if some generous donor gives some boats and motor launches for the inauguration (if possible) of an " All-India Kailas-Manasarovar Club."

CHAPTER IX

MISCELLANEOUS

The Holy Manas provides fine caves on her shores near Gossul and Cherkip gompas for hermits, and fine camping grounds and good sites here and there for Tibetans to build monasteries and houses. It is marshy at certain places, and rocky or sandy at others. One comes across boulders as smooth and round as pebbles, and also slabs as finely cut and shaped as slates. It is warm on the Gossul side and very cold on other sides. Inspite of the existence of hot springs the Chiu hill side is very cold. From one monastery the Manas presents a fine view of her northern neighbour, the Kailas, and from another she completely keeps it out of sight, while from a third monastery the Rakshas Tal is presented beautifully. There are some lakelets and lagoons scattered all round the Lake, like Yushup tso on the south-west, Tseti tso on the west, Kurkyal Chhungo, Sham tso and Ding tso on the north and north-east. In Tibetan scriptures Kurkyal Chhungo is described as the head of Manasarovar, set apart for *devatas* or gods to bathe in. In winter shepherds flock to her shores and in summer they move to the upper parts of the valleys. Indians hold a market on one side and the Nepalese on the other.

Certain monasteries are owned by Ladakh, others by Bhutan, some by Taklakot, and still others are affiliated to the Universities or monasteries of Eastern Tibet. Several paths from different parts of the world converge to this holy spot. It would be no exaggeration if I style this region as the cynosure of the world, for both the Buddhists and the Hindus, consisting of nearly 70 crores of souls, look upon Kailas and Manasarovar as the holiest of regions.

One cannot generally escape or get away without noticing a tragic spectacle here and there in the Manasarovar region. It is, for example, a pathetic sight to see hundreds of fish frozen and crushed in the swimming posture under the transparent ice (as at the mouth of the Gyuma chhu); or a whole flock or group of swans with their young ones frozen to death and sandwiched on the ever-changing mysterious Lake; or scores of new-born lambs and kids frozen to death in a shepherd camp on a single cold night, for winter is the yeaning season of sheep and goats. Sometimes groups of *kiyangs* are frozen to death on all fours, in the deep snows.

One peculiarity with the Lake is that at times when there are high waves near the shores the middle is calm and clear like a mirror reflecting the silvery dome of the Kailas if seen from the southern side or the Mandhata's giant heads if seen from the N.E. On full-moon nights, with the full-moon overhead, the scene is simply indescribable. At sunset the whole of the Kailas range on the north becomes a fiery region all of a sudden, throwing an observer into a spell of trance, and by the time he returns to consciousness he sees only the silvery peak in his front. On another occasion at the time of sunset the whole of the Mandhata catches fire and terrible flames with rolling columns of smoke rise in the west, only to be buried very soon into the depths of abysmal darkness. Sometimes the morning sun gilds the Kailas and Mandhata peaks or pours forth molten gold on the Holy Lake. On another occasion the whole of the Kailas-Manas region is completely covered with a thick blanket of snow from head to foot, making it impossible to point out which is which. One cannot tell a house from a tent, or the Lake from the land. One cannot distinguish the ground from the pit, or the mound from the bush. A moonlit night with a clear sky beggars description and one becomes simply spell-bound. Perhaps moonlight is brightest on the Tibetan plateau. Now you have scorching sun; the next moment hails and snow fall copiously; and shortly after having a nap and coming out of your room you will see a clear blue sky and bright sun above and a bed of pearl-like hails and white snow on the ground. Hence the oft-quoted Hindi couplet:

"मानसरोवर कौन परसे। बिन बादल हिम बरसे।"

"Who can approach Manasarovar where snow falls without clouds?" Such phenomena form sufficient material for the ecstatic outbursts of a poet.

Thus the Kailas-Manas region engages the attention of a person of any calling or profession—whether he be a poet or a painter, a physicist or a chemist, a botanist or a zoologist, a geologist or a surveyor, a geographer or a historian, a hunter or a sportsman, a skater or a skier, a physiologist or a psychologist, an ethnologist or a sociologist, a pilgrim or a tourist, a hermit or a householder, a clergyman or a tradesman, a treasure-hunter or a spirit-hunter, a theist or an atheist, a scholar or a politician, young or old, man or woman.

Now with waves rising up to the sky and roaring as in an ocean, and now presenting a perfectly still clear-blue sheet of water mirroring the moon and the stars and the Kailas or the Mandhata ; now like a sheet of gold in the morning sun, and now like a mass of molten silver in the full-moon light ; now rocking the Kailas and the Mandhata on her gentle ripples as in a cradle ; now calm, serene, and silent even like the space beyond, and now disturbed and roaring, dashing and lashing the shores ; sometimes raising tempestuous winds flinging even the sheep and goats in the surroundings ; now a beautiful blue and now a hard white mass, Lake Manasarovar, with her hundreds of *Avataras* and myriads of changing forms, offers an enigma to the puny self-conceited human being to think, meditate, and perhaps ultimately to fail to comprehend all these. All hail, oh Manas, Lake of the Royal Sages and Swans ! Victory to Thee !

EPILOGUE

One can spend days and nights together like so many minutes, watching the weird grandeur, splendour, and majesty of the sacred Kailas peak without being tired, or in peaceful meditation and contemplation, by the side of the turquoise-blue surface of the charming Lake Manasarovar, lulled by her awe-inspiring solemnity. One breathes more happily and with greater ease ; one feels real pleasure in life, and yearns to remain sailing indefinitely on the fascinating blue depths and the sacred waves. Discoveries in the domain of geology or geography of the Mount Kailas or study of the hydrographic relation of this unique Lake to lakes similarly situated in other parts of the world are no doubt extremely pleasant pastimes and may be attempted by a person of an average intellectual calibre ; but the inner joy which one feels when one is face to face with an object of supernatural beauty and eternal charm, such as is presented by this summit under a cupola of perpetual snow, where, according to Hindu traditions, Shiva (the Universal Spirit) abides permanently with His Divine Consort Parvati (the personification of *Prakriti* or Nature) and where, in terms of the Tibetan scriptures, the Buddha resides with his hierarchy of 500 Bodhisattvas, may be better described by one more gifted poetically and æsthetically disposed than the author. How could Kailas and Manasarovar be the objects of Divine honour from two religions so different as Hinduism and Buddhism, unless it be that their overpowering beauty and charm have not only so appealed to but made an indelible impression on the human mind, that they seemed to belong rather to heaven than to earth! Even the first view from the Gurla pass or from the hills on the shore causes one to burst into tears of joy at the magnificent landscape; a more intimate association undoubtedly throws one into mystic trances, when one feels nearer the Divine Presence than at any other time. The author feels that if he has been able to stimulate interest in any of his readers to undertake this very educative and wholesome journey to this abode of Bliss (Kailas and Manasarovar) in the region of snows (Himalayas) and to feel that inner joy which is surely to be felt by every mortal like himself, his labours will have been amply rewarded. Besides, if some devotee, having himself been inspired by the August Presence, can hand over the Torch of Illumination to his fellow brothers, the gratifying reflection of having originated and perpetuated this chain of inspiration will fill the author with supreme satisfaction—a natural and legitimate result of the fulfilment of a noble and self-imposed mission of serving humanity.

EXPLORATION IN TIBET

PART II

New Light on the Sources of the Four Great Rivers

ॐ

Introduction

Kangri Karchhak—the Tibetan *Kailas Purana*—says that the four great rivers called (1) Langchen* Khambab,† or the Elephant-mouthed river (Sutlej), on the west, (2) Singi Khambab, or the Lion-mouthed river (Indus), on the north, (3) Tamchok Khambab, or the Horse-mouthed river (Brahmaputra), on the east, and (4) Mapcha Khambab or the Peacock-mouthed river (Karnali), on the south, have their sources in Tso Mapham, the lake unconquerable (Manasarovar). According to some other Tibetan traditions these four rivers take their sources from the Holy Kailas and have 500 tributaries each.

There had long been a controversy over the sources of these rivers, till matters were taken to have been set at rest by Dr. Sven Hedin's verdict in 1907-1908. I had the good fortune in 1928 to travel in Western Tibet on a visit to the Holy Kailas and Manasarovar. I went from Srinagar (Kashmir) through Ladakh, Demchok, Gartok, Tirthapuri, Gyanima Mandi, round Kailas and Manasarovar,

* The word 'lang' means 'bull,' and the word 'langchen' means 'elephant.'

† The word 'Khamba' (coming from the mouth of) is also used in its stead. Pronunciation of several Tibetan words varies from district to district and sometimes altogether different terms are used.

to Taklakot, again to Gartok, and back to Rishikesh by the Niti pass. In 1935 I made a second journey from Bhairavghati (Gangotri), by the Jelukhaga pass,* to Tuling, Gyanima Mandi, Kailas, Manasarovar, and back to Rishikesh by the Damjan-Niti pass. In 1936-37 I travelled from Almora by the Lipu Lekh pass and returned by the same route. During the third visit I stayed for a full year in the Thugolho monastery, on the southern shore of the Manasarovar, when I had the rare opportunity of visiting the Sources of the Four Great Rivers of the Holy Lake. In 1938 I visited those places again from Almora by the Lipu Lekh pass and returned by the same route. I feel therefore that I have the right to say something about the verdict of Sven Hedin regarding the sources of the Sutlej, the Brahmaputra, and the Indus.

At the very outset, I would like to ask geographers, geologists, and surveyors as to how the source of a particular river is to be fixed. If the river in question happens to have more than one headstream, which of them is to be considered the main river? Is it decided by the quantity of water that it brings down or by the length of the particular headstream, or is the source located from the traditions of the local people? If all the three factors are together to be taken into consideration, it would be impossible to locate the sources of the four great rivers of the Holy Kailas and Manasarovar, and other Himalayan rivers, inasmuch as none of the headstreams fulfils all the three conditions. If all the

* Also known as 'Sangchok la.'

17. A Pool of water in frozen Manasarovar [See page 22

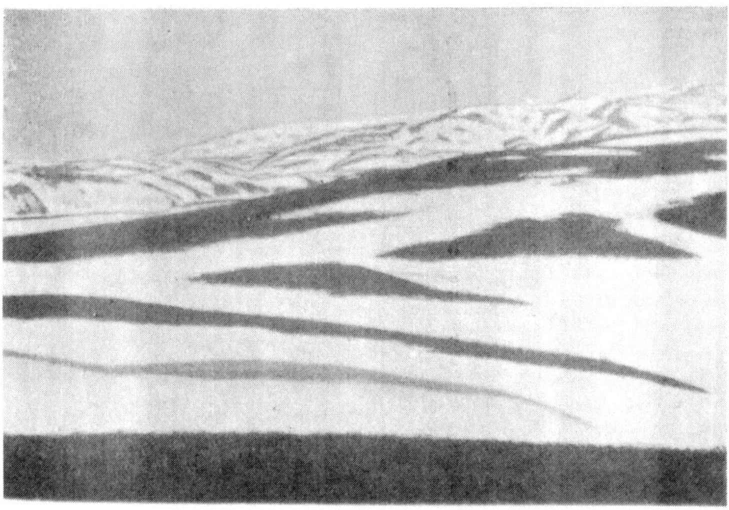

18. Zebra-like Diposits of Snow on southern shores of Rakshas Tal [See page 30

19. Gukung, Cave-village near Teklakot [*See page 41*

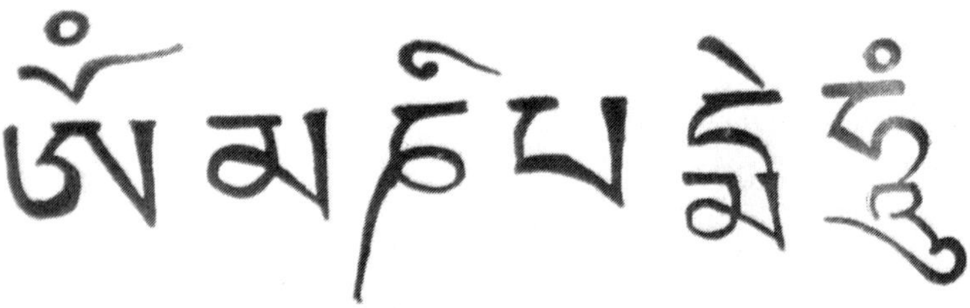

20. *Om ma ni pad me hum* [*See page 50*

21 *Tanka*, Tibetan Coin—
obverse and reverse [*See page 69*

three conditions are not fulfilled, which of them should be given the greatest weight?

The Sutlej, the Indus, the Brahmaputra, and the Karnali are considered sacred by the Tibetans, and their sources are regarded as even more sacred. In Tibet it is the custom to erect monuments in holy places and on the tops of passes wherefrom a holy place is first seen. The monument may take the form of a *chhorten* (a pagoda-like structure) *mani*-wall (a wall on which *mani*-stones or slabs are kept), some *mani*-stones or slabs (on which the Tibetan sacred *mantra*, *Om ma ni pad me hum*, is carved), cairns, coloured flags and festoons of rags, or at least heaps of stones (known as *laptche* in Tibetan). So it is not strange to expect such holy things at the sources of the four great rivers of the Holy Manasarovar ; Sven Hedin too gives detailed descriptions of them at the source of the Indus, at the spring Langchen Khambab on the banks of the Tag tsangpo, at the spring Chakko (its correct name is Chhumik Thungtol) and at several other places, as given below. " Up on the slab of rock stand three tall cairns and a small cubical *lhato* containing votive pyramids of clay. And below the *lhato* is a quadrangular *mani*, with hundreds of red flagstones, some covered with fine close inscriptions, some bearing a single character 20 inches high. On two the wheel of life was incised, and on another a divine image, which I carried off as a souvenir of the source of the Indus.

" Our guide said that the source Singi-kabab was reverenced because of its divine origin. When travellers reached this place or any other part of the upper Indus, they scooped up water with their hands, drank of it, and sprinkled their faces and heads with it.''*

"Langchen-kamba is a small side-valley on the right, from which robbers are wont to sally forth against defenceless travellers. Just below the valley a spring bubbles forth with crystal-clear water at a temperature of 38°. It is considered holy, and is marked by a pole bedecked with rags and streamers like a scare-crow. This spring is also called Langchen-kamba.

"A little further down the spring Chakko stands on a steep slope on the right bank, and its water (40·3°) is collected in a round pit 3 feet deep. A wall is erected about it, covered with flat stones, on which figures of Buddha and holy texts are carved. Leaves from the holy scriptures are thrust between the stones of the wall, and streamers and rags fly from a pole. Through the water, clear as a mirror, could be seen blue and red beads, two inferior turquoises, some shells, and other trash, thrown in as offerings by pious pilgrims. The water is supposed to have miraculous powers. Murmuring prayers, our guide filled a wooden bowl with water and poured it over the head and mane of his horse to protect it from wolves.''†

When Sven Hedin describes the source of the Brahmaputra, he however makes no mention of any such holy symbols, which are so very common in Tibet.

* Sven Hedin, 'Trans-Himalaya,' Vol. II, p. 212.

† *Op. cit.*, pp. 105, 106.

CHAPTER I

SOURCE OF THE BRAHMAPUTRA

According to Tibetan traditions, the source of the Brahmaputra lies not in the Kubi glaciers as claimed by Sven Hedin, but in the Chema-yungdung glaciers. While locating the sources of the Indus and the Sutlej, Sven Hedin tries to refer to Tibetan traditions in support of his findings, though he has not faithfully adhered to them in finally fixing the source of the Sutlej. But, unfortunately, all the quotations which Sven Hedin cites are from Chinese geographers and not even a single direct reference is made to any Tibetan work. Inspite of the fact that none of the Chinese geographers have even mentioned the name of the Kubi, Sven Hedin persists in making the Kubi the principal branch of the Tamchok Khambab. We cannot give greater prominence to Chinese geographers than to the Tibetans themselves on such questions concerning Tibet. Some of the Chinese geographers themselves place the source of the Brahmaputra in the Chema-yungdung. Let me quote Sven Hedin's own remarks, "We have seen that *some* of the Chinese writers*

* Special attention of the reader is drawn to the italicised passages in the quotations from Sven Hedin. The italics are the author's.

make the Chema the principal branch, coming from Tamchok-kabab, others say that Chema is only a tributary joining Kubi. *In all instances, both western and eastern, the Kubi-tsangpo has, however, been almost ignored. The Chinese authorities do not mention its name*, although at least in one case it is called the Yere-tsangpo. Only Kawaguchi seems to have heard its name Kubi-chu."*

When the question of the source of the Brahmaputra comes in, he does not give any Tibetan authority, except for a vague quotation from the 'Elements of Hydrography,' by the Chinese author Chi Chao Nan (1762), which runs thus, "Langchen-kabab (mountain) lies south-east of Kailas. On the east of this mountain stands the Tamchok-kabab mountain which is the source of Tamchok-kabab or the Brahmaputra."†

"When the Chinese author informs us that east of Langchen-kabab lies Tamchok-kabab, which is the source of the river Yere-tsangpo (Brahmaputra), we must admit that his description is quite in accordance with the truth, *as I, the first European to visit this country, have myself discovered*......And that the Tage-tsangpo was at one time considered by the Tibetans to be the headwater of the Sutlej is apparent from the fact that its name, Langchen-kamba, is still applied to the upper of the two sacred source streams in the valley of the Tage-tsangpo."‡

Even this single quotation gives more support to my findings than to those of Sven Hedin, because

* Sven Hedin, 'Southern Tibet,' Vol. I, p. 118.
† 'Trans-Himalaya,' Vol. II, p. 183.
‡ *Op. cit.*, p. 185.

the Chema-yungdung glaciers are east of and nearer to the Knaglung kangri glaciers (the source of the Tag), whereas the Kubi kangri glaciers (where Sven Hedin places the source of the Brahmaputra) are on the south-east of Kanglung glaciers, and not on the east, as has been mentioned by the Chinese author, whose authority Sven Hedin cites in his support.

Taking the Tibetan traditions into account, there is a monument (called Tamchok Khambab Chhorten) at the source of the Brahmaputra near the Chema-yungdung glaciers, shown to me by my Tibetan guide. There is a big boulder about 12 feet high, on the top of which are the footprints of a Buddhistic deity, and over the footprints a small hut has been erected with loose stone-walls and roof, with the horns of a wild yak placed on the top. Out of the two clay-made divine images kept in this small shrine, I carried away one (with the consent of my guide) as a souvenir of the real source of the Brahmaputra, which I visited on June 17 and 18, 1937. Adjacent to the boulder are three *donkhangs* (Tibetan *dharmashalas* or rest houses), of which one was roofed. My guide told me that the Nyakora (meaning, *tirtha-yatri* or pilgrim) tribe of nomads go over there for yak-hunting at the end of summer, as it abounds in a good many wild yaks. All round the boulder are hundreds of cairns.

The Chinese map of the Ta-ch 'ing (1744 A.D.) prepared by Dutreuil de Rhins has very correctly located the source of the Brahmaputra. His lake ' Djima Young rong ' must be the network of the several moraine lakes (which the Chinese geographers might have noted as one continuous lake from a distance) in the upper course of the river Chema-yungdung, and the " Mt. Goumang, corresponds exactly to the Chema-yungdung-pu," as has been rightly suggested by Sven Hedin. This Chema-yungdung-pu massive could be seen from a distance but Mt. Tamtchouk Kabab cannot be seen from a distance and can be seen only when one actually goes right up to the Chema-yungdung-pu, since the Mt. Tamtchouk Kabab is about 1½ or 2 miles west of the pu. This mount corresponds to the Tamchok Khambab Kangri of my sketch of the actual sources of the Brahmaputra, so very faithfully indeed that the Chinese geographers of the Ta-ch 'ing placed the Mt. Tamtchouk beyond the Chema-yungdung-pu though they have not actually visited the place. They have not connected the Mt. Tamtchouk Kabab to the stream at the Mt. Goumang, perhaps because they have not actually seen the place. Herein lies the reliability of their work! It was done similarly in the case of the source of Indus, Mt. Senghe Kabab, wherefrom no stream was shown coming out, since the Chinese writers did not actually visit the place. The only mistake that the Ta-ch 'ing committed is that it placed the Tamchok Khambab north of Goumang instead of on the west. This mistake is excusable in view of the fact that the Chinese geographers had not been actually to the place but got some information from the local people. So Sven Hedin need not be surprised if the little stream that flows into the lake Djima Young rong is not joined upwards with the Mt. Tamchouk Kabab, in the map.

The Chinese Civil Officer J. Klaproth (1840) writes that the Brahmaputra takes its source in the Tamchok Khambab snow-mountain from out of a little lake called ' Djimagoungroung,' situated east of the Langchen Khambab or the source of the Sutlej. ' Djimagoungroung ' is the corrupt form of Chema-yungdung. So, the Chinese geographer Klaproth correctly places the source of the Brahmaputra in the Chema-yungdung. I too came across several moraine lakes in the bed of the Chema-yungdung as well as in that of the Angsi, when I visited the actual source of the Brahmaputra. There are also one or two small lakelets in the Chema-yungdung-pu glaciers themselves, a little up the tongue where there are huge debris. Yet, Sven Hedin twists Klaproth's plain and correct statements in order to support his own views, and then accuses d'Anville with misunderstanding the Chinese hydrography. Sven Hedin writes, " So far as I could see the course of the river Chema-yundung no lake was visible.....He (d'Anville) seems so far to have misunderstood the Chinese hydrography, that he has placed the name Yarou Dsancpou ou Tsanpou R. along the river which corresponds to Chema-yundoung."*

D'Anville, in his map of 1733 A.D., rightly placed the source of the Brahmaputra in the Chema-yungdung (his Yarou Dsancpou). Commenting on it, Sven Hedin says, " If d'Anville had only placed the name Yarou Dsancpou along this last-mentioned branch (Kubi), his map would have been correct in

* Sven Hedin, ' Southern Tibet,' Vol. I, p. 94.

this point."* How queer and unjust are his wishes and remarks! Since *yaru* means 'upper' in the Tibetan language and since the Chema-yungdung is the upper of the two rivers, it is the Chema-yungdung that must be the Brahmaputra but not the Kubi!

Lloyd and Gerard write, "The Brahmaputra is named Tanjoo Khampa, or Erechoomboo, and one of its streams takes its rise to the south-east of Manasarowar."† At another place Gerard remarks that "*One stream, which is reckoned the principal, rises south-east of Mansurowur, and there are others from the eastward.*"‡ Indeed this principal stream must certainly be our Chema-yungdung and the 'others from the eastward' must necessarily be the Kubi and others. So, according to Gerard, the Kubi is only a tributary but never the principal stream.

Henry Strachey (1846) very correctly describes the Chema-yungdung to be the Brahmaputra. The valley of the Chema-yungdung is covered with white sands from the source down to a distance of about ten miles. The white sands (*chema*) of the river are very conspicuous and could be seen from long distances as if there had been a fresh snowfall. As he gives graphic descriptions of the sands of the Chema-yungdung it is very probable that Strachey might have got first-hand information from some authentic Tibetan sources. Even in this case, Sven Hedin summarily dismisses Strachey's findings most

* 'Southern Tibet,' Vol. II., p. 220.

† Narrative of a Journey, etc., by Sir W. Lloyd and Capt. Alex. Gerard's Account of an attempt, etc............London 1840, Vol. II, p. 186.

‡ *Ibid.*

peremptorily hiding his face from truth. Here is Sven Hedin, " Here the confusion comes in : The Tamchok-kamba rising from a place called Chema-yundung. Where then is Tamchok-kabab or the Horse river situated? Chema-yundung may easily be the name of a sandy region, but the river that flows through it is not Tamchok-kamba but Chema-yundung." If we are to argue like this, the river which flows out of his Kubi glaciers can only be the Kubi tsangpo, as he himself puts it; how can it be, I ask, the Tamchok Khambab? " And the source of this river is a glacier, or perhaps several glaciers in the mountain called Chema-yundung-pu. In this particular point *even the vague hydrography of Kawaguchi is better than Henry Strachey's.*" How unjust and unfair it is on the part of Sven Hedin to compare the great geographer Strachey with Kawaguchi, who was incapable of holding anything but crude geographical notions, *viz.*, that the circumference of Manasarovar was 200 miles, that he had a good drink of the Ganges water, at the spring Chhumik Thungtol, on the east of Manasarovar, and so on! A mere incidental mention of the name of the Kubi by Kawaguchi is good enough for Sven Hedin to cite in order to explode the most authentic and first-hand information of Strachey and to support his own views!

In his book ' Three Years in Tibet,' Ekai Kawaguchi writes that he crossed the river Kyang-chu first " which was about four hundred and fifty yards wide at places, while it narrowed to sixty yards or so at others,"* and three or four days later

* P. 104.

he crossed the Tamchok Khanbab, the width of which "was not more than a little over a mile."* Then after about three days' journey he crossed the Chema-yungdung-gi-chu, which was a hundred and eighty yards wide and was so deep that he had to swim across.† This was on his onward journey to the Holy Lake.

On his return journey from Kailas, Kawaguchi writes, he "finally reached the lower course of the river Chema-yungdung, where I had narrowly escaped drowning a short time before."‡ After two days' further journey, at the rate of 25 miles a day, from the Chema, "we reached the Brahmaputra, known in this region as Martsan-gi-chu or Kobei-chu according to the districts which it traversed. The lordly river was quite shallow and could be crossed without trouble, and I did so as before on the yak's back."§ After five or six days' further march from the Brahmaputra, Kawaguchi writes, "I found the familiar Kyang-chu river, which I was delighted to see."|| "I crossed the river about nine miles above the place where I had crossed it on the previous occasion."¶ Fifteen days after, he again "crossed the Brahmaputra."**

The reader may note from Kawaguchi's map that there are only two rivers which are cut by his route on his onward and return journey from Kailas,

* P. 110.
† Pp. 120, 121.
‡ P. 184.
§ P. 185.
|| P. 195.
¶ P. 196.
** P. 208.

besides a third one which is definitely the Brahmaputra. Of the two he gave the name ' Kyang chu R' to the first one. Now comes the question as to what might be the unnamed river? It must be either the Brahmaputra, which he calls ' Tamchok Khanbab ' on his onward journey and ' Martsan-gi-chu or Kobei-chu ' on his return journey, or the ' Chema-yungdung.' If it is argued that this is the Brahmaputra, where then is the Chema-yungdung which was so deep and broad that he had to swim a long way to cross it, and in which he was drifted away and narrowly escaped drowning? Indeed, he did show on his map the Kyang-chu, a much shallower and smaller river than the Chema ; why then did he not indicate the river Chema, by far the longer and the bigger one? If it is argued that the unnamed river in his map is the Chema itself, how was it that he omitted to give the Tamchok Khanbab which was one mile broad and the beach on the eastern side was two and a half miles broad and that on the western side half as much? So from his map and writings it is evident that his hydrography and topography of this area is hopelessly vague, confusing, and misleading. Certainly, he must have heard the names ' Martsan-gi-chu,' ' Kobei,' and ' Tamchok Khanbab,' but having made a mess of all these, he confused the Chema with the others ; because he writes that after crossing the Chema he crossed the Brahmaputra, which he called Martsan-gi-chu or Kobei. But the Kobei is not at all called Martsan-gi-chu, and the one he did actually cross was not the Martsan-gi, as, it is stated by him, some days later he crossed the Kyang-chu again

Either by mistake or through being misinformed, Kawaguchi incidentally mentioned the Kobei and the Martsan-gi-chu to be the Brahmaputra. Sven Hedin gives a big name ' hydrography '—with a nullifying adjective ' vague '—to the single line of the meagre and wrong information of Kawaguchi. It is this ' vague hydrography ' that Sven Hedin exultantly brings forward in order to ' explode ' the most authentic information of the great geographer Strachey and to support his own theory that the Kobei is the main Brahmaputra !

It may be interesting to note here that the lower course of the river Chema-yungdung is also called Martsang tsangpo or the Tamchok Khambab even much above Shamsang where the Kubi joins the Chema. This goes to prove that the Chema-yungdung is the principal branch of the Brahmaputra.

Sven Hedin's enthusiasm for fame seems to have got the better of him, thereby leading him to a deliberate suppression of facts. It is for the geographers to conduct a thorough investigation into the truth of the matter and test the validity of Sven Hedin's claims. Sven Hedin further remarks, " It is not surprising that Strachey's informant knew only the Chema-yundung and consequently believed that it was the source of the great Tsangpo. For the ordinary road over Tamlung-la touches Chema-yundung but not at all the principal river, which is Kubi-tsangpo. The nomads prefer the grass of the Chema-yundung which is more abundant and easier to get at. *And there may, perhaps, be Tibetans, who really regard the Chema-yundung as the source of the Tsangpo*, in which case, however, the Tamchok-kabab would have to be placed at Chema-yundung-pu, which is not the case.''*

When Sven Hedin could find out so many details about the Chema-yungdung, is it not really surprising to note that he could not find out the lakes in the Chema (that were noted by the Chinese geographers), and that he did not care to go to the Chema for making fuller investigations? It seems also that Sven Hedin had studied the Chinese geographers, only after he had fixed the source in the Kubi. Had he studied the Chinese geographers before he went to Tibet he would have certainly agreed with them and would have placed the source of the Brahmaputra in the Chema, as I did. Since he had at first fixed his source of the Brahmaputra in the Kubi before consulting the Chinese geographers, he had perforce to struggle hard against the Chinese findings and strive vigorously to twist their records for the support of his findings.

Graham Sandberg was quite right in describing the Chema-yungdung as the real source of the Brahmaputra. But Sven Hedin disposes of his findings as being incorrect and consoles himself by passing some shallow remarks and at the same time claiming himself to be the first discoverer of the source of the Brahmaputra.

Somehow, Nain Singh also makes the Chema-yungdung the principal branch of the Tamchok Khambab.

Whether Major Ryder got actual information or whether he simply conjuctured, in either case, he

* Sven Hedin, 'Southern Tibet,' Vol. II, p. 224.

was perfectly correct and justified in making the Chema-yungdung the main river of the Tamchok Khambab or the Brahmaputra, and the Kubi only a tributary.

The fact underlying the whole affair is that Sven Hedin could not get an opportunity to go to the Chema-yungdung. He thought he would be able to investigate the sources of the Sutlej and the Indus also on the same basis (by measuring the quantities of water) as in the case of the Brahmaputra and never even dreamt that he would miserably fail to do so, and that he would be forced to fall back on the Tibetan traditions to support his findings. To his great disadvantage and disappointment the Tibetan Government were putting obstacles in the freedom of his movements. As a matter of fact he had to exercise great tact and elude the Tibetan officers at Parkha (midway between Kailas and Manasarovar), so that he might get an opportunity of visiting the source of the Indus from the northern side of Kailas. What he had contrived to achieve his object was this. He despatched the whole of his caravan, from Khaleb to Gartok by the *tasam* (high-road) with instructions to march very slowly and himself went to the Singi Khambab, telling the Tibetan officers that he was going only for a few days' excursion into the mountains on the north and that he would soon come back to join his main party by the *tasam;* so he had neither choice nor time to fix the source of the Indus and the Sutlej after duly measuring the quantity of water which the different headwaters discharged and then to proceed to the head of the biggest of them. Nor could he willingly let the results of the work he had done at the Kubi go in vain. Besides other things, he did not like to spend much time at the Singi Khambab, in measuring the water in the different head-streams and in going to the source of the biggest, because he was not certain as to which of the two streams—the Singi or the Gartong—would carry more water, since he had yet to make the actual measurements. If the latter happened to carry more water, as it does oftentimes (which fact I gathered from local information), he would have to place the source of the Indus at the head of the Gartong chhu, according to his " theory of greater quantity of water " (as in the case of the Brahmaputra), and consequently the results he had worked out at the Singi Khambab would be in vain. So he had to fall back solely on the Tibetan traditions and rest content with the remarks that " The problem cannot be settled in any more satisfactory way than to accept the Tibetan view," and " Any attempt to persuade the Tibetans would fail, for it had tradition in its favour." Has this sapient explorer, who shows off his broad-mindedness towards other civilizations, cared a straw for the Tibetan traditions in fixing the source of the great river Brahmaputra, one of the four holiest rivers of the Tibetans?

Sven Hedin would have served the cause of truth better if he had frankly admitted the difficulties of deciding upon suitable and consistent criteria for fixing the sources of these rivers instead of struggling desperately for the achievement of the coveted honour of being the first and original discoverer of the sources of these three rivers. By giving preference to the quantity of water in the case of the Brahmaputra, tradition in the case of the Indus, and far-fetched tradition and length in the case of the Sutlej, he has not hesitated to sacrifice mercilessly all consistent, reasonable, and uniform procedure which has to be adopted in dealing with such important problems. Had not Sven Hedin been compelled to go by a devious route for securing guides and yaks, he would certainly have gone to the head of the Chema-yungdung, and, would, I am sure, have, without any hesitation whatsoever, fixed the source of the Brahmaputra in the Chema-yungdung glaciers, in confirmation of the reports of the nomads and the people of Bongba he would meet on his way. And later on he would have found that the Chinese geographers including Chi Cho Nan and Klaproth, Rhins, D'Anville, Lloyd and Gerard, Strachey, Sandberg, Nain Singh, Major Ryder, and others were quite right in placing the source of the Brahmaputra in the Chema-yungdung. Little did he dream that a lay monk, who would be on a spiritual mission at the Holy Lake on several occasions, possessing none of the facilities and equipment that the Western explorers always have at their disposal, would upset his theories in 1937 !

The following lines from Sven Hedin will speak for themselves regarding the hollowness of his arguments and the helpless way in which he begs the question : " I cannot, however judge in this case, as I never went up to the source of the Chema-yundung-chu...*The problem will have to be solved in the future and the very source of the Chema-yundung, even if well-known by certain*

22. Similing Gompa of Taklakot [*See page 51*

23. Gyanima Mandi [*See page 63*

24. Mount Kailas on a full-moon night [*See page 72*

25. A *laptche*, with flags, streamers, *mani*-stones, yak-horns, etc., near Tirthapuri [*See page 81*

Tibetan tribes, has not yet been discovered by any European."* Thus Sven Hedin consoles himself, in his inability to visit the Chema-yungdung under forced circumstances, by saying that it has not yet been discovered by any other European. Further, while admitting that "The problem will have to be solved in the future," he, at the same time, claims himself to be the first discoverer of the real source of the Brahmaputra! Some travellers previous to Sven Hedin had seen the Chema-yungdung from a distance and located it as the source of the Brahmaputra; even so did Sven Hedin simply see the Kanglung kangri from a distance and fix the source of the Tag (and hence the Sutlej) in it. If the actual visiting of the glacier is a necessary condition, Sven Hedin too cannot claim to have discovered the source of the Sutlej in the Kanglung kangri since he did not actually go to the glacier and make a thorough investigation as in the case of Brahmaputra, for there is more than one glacier in the Kanglung group as in the Kubi.

A little further Sven Hedin says, "The most comfortable and shortest way to Tag-la or Tamlung-a would have been to follow the course of the Chema-yundung and its tributary Angsi-chu to the west, which would have spared us the Marnyak-la; but I had to take the longer and more difficult way to the north to reach a Camp where new guides and yaks could be had, as my men from Shamsang had to return from here."† "The Chema-yundung

* Sven Hedin, 'Southern Tibet,' Vol. II, p. 248.
† *Op. cit.*, p. 264.

seems to be a few miles longer than the Kubi. So in length and absolute height the western branch is no doubt more distinguished than the eastern. But the volume of water is overwhelming in the latter, and all who in future see both rivers will agree with the Chinese and Tibetans, as I did, and call the Kubi-tsangpo the source of the Brahmaputra."*

Inspite of the fact that the Chema-yungdung is the traditional source and is more distinguished by its length and absolute height than the Kubi, Sven Hedin overlooks all these points, and gives preference to the volume of water and puts the source in the Kubi glaciers. But in fixing the sources of the Sutlej and the Indus he gives absolutely no place or consideration whatsoever to the volume of water. Can anybody pronounce such findings to be scientific?

" Sven Hedin had moreover an advantage over Moorcroft and Strachey, in that he was a Tibetan linguist and on friendly terms with the Tibetans."† As such Sven Hedin should have at least pondered over the meaning of the word Tamchok Khambab. *Ta*—horse, *amchok*—ears, *khambab*—coming from the mouth of. So the meaning of the word Tamchok Khambab is 'Horse-ears-mouthed rivers.'‡ The

* *Ibid.*

† Burrard and Hayden, *op. cit.*, p. 229.

‡ This is the derivation of the term 'Tamchok Khambab' given to me by some Nyakora nomads on the spot. During my recent visit to Tibet one learned Lama of Taklakot told me that the word 'Tamchok' means superior or celestial horse. Let me plainly confess here that I am not a master of Tibetan language though I know a little of it and that I had often to depend upon my interpreters. So even if the first meaning of the term is not correct, it does not materially affect my general findings.

sources of the four great rivers are located by Tibetans in certain springs, to which they attribute the appearance of the mouths of various animals just as the Hindus call the source of the Ganges '*Goumukh*' or Cow-mouth. There are two glaciers, called Chema-yungdung-pu and the Tamchok Khambab kangri with a broad-faced peak separating them. The monument or the shrine is situated on the left bank of the Brahmaputra (where it is called Chema-yungdung chhu) between these two glaciers and opposite the broad-faced peak. There is a dry spring near by, which is said to contain water in the summer and rainy seasons. The two glaciers are the two ears, and the boulder is the mouth. Both these glaciers together go by the general name of Chema-yungdung-pu, or simply Chema-yungdung. The distance between the two glaciers is about 1½ or 2 miles. A little to the north or north-west of the Tamchok Khambab glaciers is another smaller glacier or snow-field behind which is the Angsi glacier.

It is really regrettable to note that Sven Hedin did not care to make inquiries from the nomads and from the Bongba pilgrims to Kailas whom he passed in the "broad open valley of the Chema-yundung river, which descends from a very extensive glacier in the south belonging to the Chema-yundung-pu massive." Besides this, he tries his level best to place the source of the Brahmaputra in the Kubi kangri glaciers by giving us facts and figures to show that the Kubi tsangpo discharges more water than the Chema-yungdung. But unfortunately he totally forgets this "theory of greater discharge of water," when he locates the sources of the Indus and the Sutlej.

Regarding the source of the Brahmaputra, Sven Hedin writes, " No other traveller had ever been in this region, and I would on no account miss the opportunity of penetrating the actual source of the Brahmaputra and fixing its position definitely...At Shamsang the source-streams meet, and below this point the united river bears the name Martsang-tsangpo. First of all, I must, of course, gauge the quantities of water in the source-streams, and, if they were nearly equal, we must be content to say that the Brahmaputra has several sources...I betook myself first, on July 8, to the point on the southern sides of the valley where two streams run together, the Kubi-tsangpo from the south-west and the Chema-yundung from the west. A short day's march further west the Chema-yundung receives the Marium-chu, which comes from the Marium-la. First the united stream was gauged, and found to discharge 1554 cubic feet of water per second, and immediately after the Chema-yundung, which discharged almost 353 cubic feet. Subtracting this from the volume of the united river, we get 1201 feet as the discharge of the Kubi-tsangpo. This river is then three and a half times as large as the Chema, and it should be remembered that the Chema also receives the water of the Marium-chu, so that its 353 cubic feet represent the united volumes of two tributaries......To arrive at the source we had only to know that the Kubi-tsangpo is far larger than the two others, so we have to follow its course up into the mountains, which none of my predecessors had done. The Tibetans also said that the Kubi was the upper course of the Martsang-tsangpo.''*

" We crossed another saddle, Sen-kamba-la, to reach the broad open valley of the Chema-yun-dung river, which descends from a very extensive glacier in the south belonging to the Chema-yun-dung-pu massive. Here were several nomad tents, and seven tents inhabited by pilgrims from Bongba stood on a rise. They were on their way with kith and kin to Kang-rinpoche to make the pilgrimage round the holy mountain. Most of the pilgrims from the far east take this southern route and return over the Marium-la.''*

In fact, according to the Tibetan tradition the source of the Chema-yungdung is the source of the Brahmaputra, and the Chema-yungdung is the actual Brahmaputra ; it is also longer than the Kubi. So whether length or traditions be taken into consideration, the source of the Brahmaputra cannot be placed in the Kubi glaciers, and must be placed in Chema-yungdung glaciers. But if one persists in placing the source of the Brahmaputra in the Kubi glaciers on the ground of its quantity of water, the present location of sources of the Indus and the Sutlej must be taken as incorrect and should, therefore, be shifted to some other places. If the sources of the rivers are to be fixed according to local traditions, as is done in the case of the Ganges and several other rivers, the source of the Brahmaputra should be shifted from the Kubi to the Chema-yungdung. So which-

*' Trans-Himalaya,' Vol. II, pp. 90, 91.

ever theory be followed, Sven Hedin cannot claim to be the discoverer of the sources of the Brahmaputra, the Indus, and the Sutlej, as he asserts thus, " If geographers had been asked in the year 1906 to point out on a large-scale map of Western Tibet the source of the Brahmaputra, they would have been considerably perplexed, and each would have laid his finger on a different place. Even those who knew Ryder's results would have given undecided answers. No one, not even Ryder himself, could have placed the points of compasses on a particular point and said 'Here.' The position of the Sutlej source would have been fixed with still greater uncertainty, and only those who knew the records would have answered that the question had not yet been decided. The source of the Indus might have been located within a narrower circle, though its radius would have measured 20 miles; but *no European had tried to reach it*, and Montgomerie's pundits had been obliged to turn back when there were still several days' journey from the source. *At last in the year 1907 I succeeded in finding my way to the sources of all three rivers.*"*

Inspite of Sven Hedin's verdict in 1907, and the subsequent acceptance of the same by Burrard of the Survey of India, the sources of the four rivers Sutlej, Indus, Brahmaputra and Karnali were, as a matter of fact, as uncertain, in the year 1936 (*i.e.*, 30 years after Sven Hedin) even as they had been in the year 1906. At last it was in the year 1937 that I succeeded in discovering the sources of these four

* *Ibid.*, p. 103.

rivers from all the points of view, namely, tradition, volume, length, and glaciers.

Here one more point conspicuously attracts our attention. On a close observation of Sven Hedin's map we note that he gives the Tibetan names of only three sub-glaciers of the Kubi-kangri group (Langtchen glacier, Absi glacier, and Ngomo-dingling glacier) but not of the Brahmaputra glacier. Brahmaputra glacier is the Indian name and certainly not the Tibetan name. Why should he particularly evade giving the Tibetan name of the Brahmaputra glacier, when he could give us the Tibetan names of the sources of the Sutlej (Ganglung glacier) and the Indus (Singi-kabab)? Is it because that Sven Hedin believed that " Providence had reserved for him the triumph of reaching the actual source of the Brahmaputra "? The Tibetan name of the Brahmaputra glacier would have given us a clue as to whether the Tibetans really consider that to be the source of the Tamchok Khambab.

If there be an impartial judge, I would stand before him and claim the trophy for having discovered the real sources of the four great rivers after actually visiting them. Except for the Tibetans themselves, I can say without fear of contradiction that I am the first to visit and discover the sources of all the four rivers simultaneously, inspite of a complete lack of the expeditional equipment which all the previous explorers had. If anybody wants to verify the validity of my findings, I am ready to accompany any expedition party and guide it to the various sources of these rivers and prove the truth of my statements to their entire satisfaction. Had Sven

Hedin cared at least to note the traditional source of the Brahmaputra, he could have very easily got the information from any nomad tent or Bongba tents which he came across on his way to Manasarovar from the Kubi. From all that I have discussed and described if one judges with an unbiassed mind, one cannot but conclude that Dr. Sven Hedin either consciously evaded the question of traditional source in the case of the Brahmaputra in order to have the sole credit of being the " first white man and European " to discover it, or made a grievous blunder in locating the source in the Kubi glaciers instead of placing it in the Chema-yungdung glaciers. My readers may hesitate to accept the first view, but I am reluctant to accept the second in view of the fact that Sven Hedin had travelled for several days amongst those tracts and amongst people most of whom very well knew the Chema-yungdung to be the real source of the Brahmaputra according to their tradition and several of whom actually go to the very source of the Brahmaputra for wild yak hunting.

Of the three headwaters of the Brahmaputra—the Kubi, the Chema-yungdung, the Angsi, and the Marium chhu—the Kubi is the biggest (3½ times the Chema), and as such its source in the Kubi glaciers should be regarded as the source of the Brahmaputra if the quantity of water is taken into account. But if length should be the deciding factor, the Chema-yungdung, which is 6 or 7 miles longer than the Kubi (which Sven Hedin himself admits), should be the main stream of the Brahmaputra. The Kubi glaciers are at a distance of nearly four short days' march from the Chema-yungdung glaciers. Then again Angsi chhu may be a bit longer than the Chema-yungdung and the Angsi glaciers also are equally massive. It seems, therefore, that we may have to shift the source of the Brahmaputra to the Angsi.

One more interesting point before I finish with the Brahmaputra. The Indian Bhotia merchants who go from the Manasarovar beyond the Kubi tsangpo* for purchase of wool, consider the Tamulung tso to be the source of the Brahmaputra, inasmuch as a stream from it flows into the Angsi chhu and subsequently into the Chema-yungdung which is considered by them to be the main stream of the Brahmaputra. As such those Indian merchants call Tamulung tso ' Brahmakund,' and consider it sacred and bathe in it.

* Bhotias call it ' Kupi chhu.'

CHAPTER II

SOURCE OF THE SUTLEJ

About the source of the Sutlej Sven Hedin writes, " The monks (of Dolchu-gompa) believe that the water comes from Langak-tso, but nevertheless they call it (the spring at Dolchu) the Langchen-kabab, the river which flows out of the mouth of the elephant."*

Here I would like to draw the attention of the reader to the following passage: " A year later I followed the old bed a day's march further west, and found at Dolchu-gompa permanent springs of abundant water, which likewise well up on the bottom of the bed. From here and all along its course through the Himalayas the Tibetans call the Sutlej Langchen-kamba, the Elephant river; the hill on which the convent Dolchu-gompa is built is supposed to bear some resemblance to an elephant, and hence the name. The spring at Dolchu is called Langchen-kabab, or the mouth out of which the Elephant river comes, just as the Brahmaputra source is the Tamchok-kabab, or the mouth out of which the Horse river comes, and the Indus source is the Singi-kabab, or the mouth from which the Lion river comes. The fourth in the series is the Mapchu-

* 'Trans-Himalaya,' Vol. II, p. 187.

kamba, the Peacock river or Karnali. *The Tibetans assert that the source of the Sutlej is at the monastery Dolchu, not in the Himalayas or the Trans-Himalaya, from which, however, it receives very voluminous tributaries.* They are also convinced that the source water of the Langchen-kamba originates from Langak-tso. And I would draw particular attention to the fact that the first of the two holy springs which pour their water into the Tage-tsangpo is also called Langchen-kamba, a proof that in old times the source was supposed to lie to the east of Tso-mavang.'' *

The above passage is characteristic of Sven Hedin's argumentation. One can note how he deduces inferences to suit his purpose. He further says, '' Worthy of notice is the circumstance that, according to the lamas of Tirtapuri, the Sutlej came from Rakas-tal, though the channel between the two lakes was dry, and therefore no water could flow out of the western lake unless through subterranian passage. Hence it seems that the monks trace back the Sutlej to Rakas-tal, inspite of climatic variations which cause the water to fail periodically.'' †

'' Colebrooke, however, adds the suggestion that the lake when it rises sufficiently may discharge its surplus water to Rakas-tal, from which the Sutlej originates......It is not enough to say that the Manasarowar is the source of the Sutlej. The largest of the streams that feed the lake is the uppermost course of the Sutlej. And as the Tage-tsangpo

* *Op. cit.*, p. 182.

† 'Trans-Himalaya,' Vol. III, p. 223.

is very much larger than all the rest, there can be no doubt where the real source lies." *

The statement of Sven Hedin that "The Tibetans assert that the source of the Sutlej is at the monastery Dolchu, not in the Himalayas or the Trans-Himalaya, from which, however, it receives very voluminous tributaries." is in consonance with and in corroboration of the *Kangri Karchhak* which describes that, "the Sutlej (Langchen Khambab) takes its rise from out of the springs in the ground, on the west of Manasarovar, at a *pagche* (distance of a day's journey) from Kailas." It is clearly written in the Tibetan scripture the *Kangri Karchhak* that the four great rivers take their rise from the four directions of the Kailas and Manasarovar, that the Langchen Khambab has its source on the west of Manasarovar but definitely not on the east of it, and that the Tamchok Khambab has its source on the east of Tso Mavang. On the face of such an unambiguous statement on the part of the Tibetans and their scriptures and with all his professed respect for the local traditions, it is hard to understand why Sven Hedin goes on shifting the source from Dulchu gompa to Rakshas Tal, then to Manasarovar and thence to the spring Langchen Khambab on the Tag tsangpo and finally to Kanglung kangri, wherefrom the Tag takes its rise. Had Sven Hedin really cared to respect Tibetan traditions how could he place the sources of both the Langchen and Tamchok Khambabs on the east of Manasarovar? Whereas in the case of Indus, he retains the source as it is

* *Op. cit.*, p. 212.

in the springs of Singi Khambab and does not trace it back to the source of any river like the Bokhar chhu into which the water of the springs flows.

According to Sherring also the actual source of the Sutlej is in the springs at Dulchu gompa. "The actual source of this river is at the monastery of Dulju where there is a large spring, though a dry channel is continued up to the Rakshas tal, and in places in this channel water is found. The local statements all agree in asserting that there is an underground flow of water throughout the entire length of this dry channel, which occasionally comes to the surface only to disappear later on. There can be no doubt, that during a season of very heavy rain and floods this dry channel would connect the source at Dulju with the Rakshas tal."*

There is yet one more issue of serious consideration for further exploration and that is as follows. Some Tibetans believe and say that the Sutlej (Langchen Khambab) disappears at Lejandak and reappears in the springs at Dulchu monastery and that is why they hold the springs at Dulchu to be the traditional source of the Sutlej according to their scriptures. But one Johar merchant at Tarchen (southern foot of Kailas) told me that he had travelled from Dulchu to Lejandak on his way to Kailas along the Sutlej in the years 1937 and 1938 and saw water flowing very slowly in it. I cannot definitely say whether he actually saw the Sutlej or mistook some other stream for the Sutlej. So the flow of water in the Sutlej from the camping

* Sherring, 'Western Tibet' (1906), pp. 284, 285.

ground Lejandak to Dulchu (a short day's march) is a matter which remains yet to be definitely investigated.

As argued by Sven Hedin in fixing the source of the Brahmaputra, if the quantity of water is taken into consideration, the source of the Sutlej cannot be placed in the Kanglung glaciers but somewhere else. Personally I prefer the local traditions in fixing the source of a river to any other considerations. But I am simply offering a suggestion in case the criterion for deciding the source of a river is changed.

About three miles down Tirthapuri, a river called Langchen tsangpo (by the same name as the Tirthapuri branch, coming from the Rakshas Tal) joins the Sutlej. When I asked my guide why this river was called Langchen tsangpo he told me that both this and the Dulchu branch went to make up the Langchen Khambab (the Sutlej) and so this branch also was called Langchen. The Langchen tsangpo carriers more water than the Tirthapuri branch. The four rivers—the Chhinku, Guni yankti, Darma yankti, and the Gyanima branch join together to form the river Langchen tsangpo. The Chhinku and the Gyanima branches carry much less water than the other two. The Guni yankti (called Chhu Minjung in Tibetan) and the Darma yankti (Chhu Minjing) taken individually carries more water each than the Tag tsangpo, where it falls into the Manasarovar. Of these two rivers, the Darma yankti carries more water. The Darma yankti taken individually also often carries more water than the Tirthapuri branch. So if the quantity of water is taken into account, the source of the Darma yankti should be the source of the Sutlej ; that is, it is in the Zanskar range near Darma pass.

Even according to Sven Hedin, the Langchen tsangpo carried 2,943 cubic feet of water per second, whereas the Tirthapuri branch (Sutlej) carried 3,009 cubic feet of water in the year 1908. In other words, the Langchen carried 66 cubic feet less than the Tirthapuri branch. Even this small difference of 66 cubic feet is due to the facts, that Sven Hedin measured the water in the Chukta, Goyak, Trokpo-shar, and Trokpo-nup just after heavy rains, whereas the water in the Sutlej, down the Langchen tsangpo was measured on a clear day. Had all the above-mentioned streams been measured under the same circumstances, certainly, even in the year 1908 Sven Hedin would have found the Langchen tsangpo carrying more water than the Tirthapuri branch. Could I get even the slightest help from any geographical society or from the Survey of India office, I would have easily measured the volume of water simultaneously on any particular day and would have shown that the Langchen carries more water than the Tirthapuri branch. Surely Sven Hedin was fully conscious of this fact, for later on he remarks that, " undoubtedly the Darma-yankti carries at certain times more water than the branch of Tirthapuri." So far as I have seen and so far as my information goes, the Langchen tsangpo carries more water than the Tirthapuri branch. Hundreds of Bhotia merchants of Johar and Khampas going to Gyamima Mandi, Tirthapuri, and Gartok every year cross these rivers Guni yankti, Darma yankti and the Tirthapuri branch, and they all testify to this effect. The streams which go to form the Langchen tsangpo, especially the Darma yankti and the Guni yankti receive large quantities of water from the monsoon in rainy season and from glaciers all the year round, whereas the northern tributaries of the Tirthapuri river receive less water from these sources. Sven Hedin himself says, "*Samtang Rangdol* (his Tibetan guide) *affirmed that this river* (Haltshor-chu or Langchen tsangpo of Survey maps) *had as large a volume of water as the Sutlej itself,* and therefore was held by some to be the present headwater of the Sutlej."*

When Henry Strachey suggests that the source of the river Darma yankti may be the source of the Sutlej, Sven Hedin disposes of the matter summarily by saying, "Shortly after, in the autumn of 1846, Henry Strachey accomplished his well-known journey to the frequently discussed lake district, turning his steps first to the Raksas-tal, which was less known, and which seemed to him more interesting, because the Sutlej ran out of its north-western corner. His examination convinced him that no visible water-course left the lake and that the only outlet he could find was through the permeable ground. But he did not deny that abundant precipitation might raise the surface of the lakes to such a degree that the surplus water might flow away through the bed still visible in the north-west. He also puts the question whether the Darma-yankti, a tributary coming from the south and joining the Sutlej of Tirthapuri may not be the true

* 'Trans-Himalaya,' Vol. III, pp. 241, 242.

26. Chema-yungdung-pu Glaciers [See page 99

27. Tamchok Khambab Chhorten [See pages 85, 99

28. Tamchok Khambab Kangri Glaciers [See page 99

29. Dulchu Gompa [See page 106

source of the Sutlej. The decision, however, he left for exact measurements. *Undoubtedly, the Darma-yankti carries at certain times more water than the branch of Tirthapuri.*"* Sven Hedin passed by this road only once and at that time measured the water of the various tributaries of the Sutlej under different circumstances and conditions, which supported his view, and even then the Tirthapuri branch carried only 66 cubic feet of water more than the Langchen tsangpo. So it is evident, he would not rely on Tibetans for accurate information; how could he then say with any certainty, "Undoubtedly the Darma-yankti carries at certain times more water than the branch of Tirthapuri."? Evidently Sven Hedin was fully aware of the fact that he took the measurements of water in the different streams under different circumstances. This shirking of the truth on the part of Sven Hedin is worth noting. No doubt Strachey left the decision for exact measurements. That is fair, and his statement was correct. Of course Sven Hedin gave the measurements; but they were taken under different conditions, and yet he disposes of Strachey's suggestion, holding his own observations to be quite correct and claiming for himself the credit of discovering the source of the Sutlej.

Sven Hedin continues, "*But if we are to move the source from one point to another according to the volume of either stream, we may as well give up the problem as unsolvable. Reckoned from the source of the Tage-tsangpo the Tirthapuri branch is the longest.*"† Here he brings into consideration

* 'Trans-Himalaya,' Vol. III, p. 221. † *Ibid.*

the length of the river and the local traditions and begs the question. But he completely overlooks both these points without any heed in the case of Brahmaputra. " Some writers define the source of the river as the point of its source, that is most remote from its mouth. Colonel George Strahan has shown that if this definition be applied to the Ganges, its source will not be Himalayan at all but will lie near Mhow in Central India at the head of the Chambal."* If the quantity of water is taken into account, the source of the famous Holy Ganges cannot be placed at Goumukh, but should be located at the Niti or the Mana pass in as much as the Alakananda, which takes its rise there is twice as big as the Bhagirathi (which comes from Goumukh) at Devaprayag where these two rivers meet.

Here is the observation of Longstaff which bears out the contention that the Darma yankti should be regarded as the true source of the Sutlej, should the quantity of water be the criterion. " On the way we forded the Darma yankti, Gun yankti, and the Chu-Naku, all rapid glacier streams with only slightly sunken beds. The former is undoubtedly, as Sir Henry Strachey suggested in 1846, the longest branch of the headwaters of the Sutlej ; while the three streams which combine to form Chu-kar (Langchen tsangpo of Survey maps and Haltshorchu of Sven Hedin) must carry a greater volume of water than the Sutlej where I forded at Tirthapuri."†

* Burrard and Hayden, *op. cit.*, p. 184.

† T. G. Longstaff, M.A., M.D., *Geographical Journal*, February 1907, p. 208.

When I had a talk with the *goba* of Tarchen about the findings of Sven Hedin regarding the sources of Tibetan rivers, he argued with me as follows : " The Trokpo-shar, which joints the Sutlej about six miles up Tirthapuri monastery is much bigger than the Sutlej itself which comes from Dulchu, as the Trokpo-shar brings large quantity of glacial water. So, why not place the source of the Sutlej in the Kailas Range, wherefrom the Trokpo-shar takes its rise?" Logically speaking the *goba's* suggestion also is certainly worth noting; for according to Sven Hedin's calculation, the stream Trokpo-shar carried 953 cubic feet of water per second, whereas the Dulchu branch carried only 661 cubic feet of water in the year 1908.

In fixing the source of the Brahmaputra, Sven Hedin gives preference to the Kubi tsangpo over the Chema-yungdung, as the Kubi is three and a half times as large as the Chema; but in the case of Sutlej he pays no heed whatever, even though the affluent Chukta is 50 times as large as the source stream of the Sutlej. Let Sven Hedin speak for himself. " The affluent Chukta falls through a gap in the erosion terrace and divides into five delta arms with thick greyish-brown foaming water above the gravelly ground. The fifth arm of this river, which rises in the Trans-Himalaya, was 58 yards broad and discharged 530 cubic feet per second. *It was, indeed, about fifty times as large as the source-stream of the Sutlej;* but the latter flows all the year round, whereas the Chukta swells up after rain but fails altogether in the cold of winter."*

* 'Trans-Himalaya,' Vol. III, p. 184.

Though the Chukta is fifty times as large as the stream of the Sutlej coming from the springs at Dulchu, Sven Hedin gives preference to the latter on the ground that the former might become dry in winter, while the latter carries the spring water from Dulchu all the year round. If the flow of water throughout the year is a necessary condition, how could Sven Hedin say that the Sutlej is coming from Rakshas Tal or Manasarovar though the channel from Dulchu to Rakshas Tal (a distance of two days' march) and the connecting channel from Manasarovar to Rakshas Tal are dry all the year round, according to his own observations or at least for the major part of the year according to the observations of his predecessors? Even the flow from the springs at Dulchu and Singi Khambab is only for a short distance, at the most for two furlongs or even less. Hence the flow of water all the year round from the spring sources, should not and could not be brought in as an argument in the case of the rivers of these regions.

If argued from the similarity of names even then the conclusion is irresistable that the Langchen tsangpo (Haltshor-chu of Sven Hedin) should be the principal headwater of the Sutlej, which we have already discussed. Nyanri gompa (the western monastery of Kailas), situated on the right bank of Lha chhu, contains two big elephant tusks, which are each 20 inches in circumference at their thicker ends and 54 inches long, and there is the famous cave called 'Langchen-phuk' (elephant-cave) near the monastery. Similarly, the Zunthulphuk gompa (eastern monastery of Kailas), situated on the right bank of the Zhong chhu (the eastern tributary of the Lha chhu) contains two elephant tusks, smaller than those in the Nyanri gompa. So why not the source of the Lha chhu in the Lhe la or Tsethi la be considered the genetic source of the Sutlej, in view of the fact that the Lha chhu carries greater quantity of water where it enters the Langak Tso than the Tag where it falls into the Tso Mavang, and in view of the fact that even in this case the traditional source remains in tact at Dulchu gompa?

According to Sven Hedin, the Lha chhu carried 280 cubic feet of water per second, a few miles up Nyanri gompa, in the year 1907. The Zhong chhu, which joins the Lha chhu is almost equally big. So the combined river along with the affluents Tarchen chhu and Khaleb chhu certainly carry over 600 cubic feet of water per second, by the time it enters the Langak Tso; whereas the Tag tsangpo brings only 397 cubic feet of water into the Manasarovar.

Sven Hedin left no stone unturned, rightly or wrongly, by all means, to assert and claim that he was the first white man to discover the sources of the three great Himalayan rivers under discussion. To support his views, in the case of Indus, he calls the small stream Bokhar chhu as Bokhar tsangpo (big river), which is not considered to be a tsangpo by the local people; in the case of Brahmaputra he calls the Kubi, a 'tsangpo'; and makes the Chema-yungdung, a 'chhu,' (which also is called tsangpo after the Angsi chhu joins it); and in the case of Langchen tsangpo (Darma yankti), which is in fact a big river he reduces it to an ordinary stream 'Haltshor-chu.' He does not even mention the name 'Langchen tsangpo' lest the very name should go against his findings and be proposed by some one as the Sutlej, on the likeness of the name 'Langchen' and the bigness of the river 'tsangpo.'

Sven Hedin did, no doubt, more exploration work in the unknown Tibet than many of his predecessors. But that is no argument why we should accept his findings about the sources of the rivers under discussion as final and correct, especially when we see quite a number of reasons against these.

I do not mean to say that the Rakshas Tal, the Manasarovar and the Tag are not in the catchment area of the Sutlej basin. My only contention is that, should the quantity of water be the criterion for deciding the source of a river, the source of the Sutlej certainly cannot be placed in the Kanglung kangri but should be placed at the head of the Darma yankti, Trokpo-shar, Chukta, or Lha chhu as the case may be. As Sven Hedin argues, should the name of the spring Langchen Khambab on the Tag be a proof that in olden days the source of the Langchen was supposed to lie to the east of Manasarovar, even on that hypothesis, the Langchen tsangpo, the principal head-stream of which is Darma yankti, must carry greater weight so as to deduce that the Langchen tsangpo is the main head-stream of the Langchen Khambab and consequently that the actual source is near the Darma pass.

Ganga Chhu (the outlet of Manasarovar into Rakshas Tal): When Sven Hedin visited the Manasarovar he found " The highest point of Ganga chhu lying more than 6½ feet above the level of Manasarowar and the bed of the Ganga chhu to be dry." I crossed the Ganga Chhu just near the Chiu gampa, about a hundred yards from the Manasarovar, on September 4, 1928. That year it was exceptionally dry, and there was very little rainfall, yet the Ganga Chhu was 3½ feet deep and the flow was very rapid. I crossed it a second time on August 21, 1935, two miles from the Rakshas Tal. The current was gentle and it was nearly 3 feet deep. I crossed it a third time half a mile from Manasarovar on September 5, 1937, and it was nearly 2½ feet deep. I again crossed the Ganga Chhu on six other occasions near the Chiu* gompa early in winter of 1937, when I was doing the circumambulations of the Holy Manasarovar. The stream of water 1½ feet deep was frozen *en block* in the bed of the Ganga Chhu. But near the hot springs (about 2 furlongs from Manasarovar) there was flowing water 6 inches deep. I followed closely the six-mile winding course of the Ganga Chhu along its left bank from the Rakshas Tal right up to the Manasarovar on April 14, 1937, and I found ice and snow throughout the bed of the Ganga Chhu, although at several places regular slow flow of water towards the Rakshas Tal was seen. The water was very muddy where the Ganga Chhu was flowing into the Rakshas Tal. I crossed the Ganga Chhu again on June 26, and July 17, 1937, when there was a flowing water about 10 inches deep. I crossed it once again for the thirteenth time on July 27, 1937,

* Also pronounced 'Jiu.'

and the water was about 16 inches deep. I crossed the Ganga Chhu at two places for the fourteenth time on August 20, 1938, firstly near the Chiu gompa about a 100 yards from the Manasarovar, where the water was 3 feet deep, and secondly over 2 furlongs down the Chiu hill (or over half a mile from the Manasarovar) where it was 21 inches deep. The current of water was sufficiently rapid. I crossed it twice again at the same places for the fifteenth time on August 26, 1938 where the water was 3½ feet and 27 inches deep respectively and the flow was rapid. During the course of these 10 years from 1928 to 1938 I crossed the Ganga Chhu in different seasons during five years and for the remaining five years enquired about the same of the Bhotia merchants who cross it annually. I was informed that there was flow of water during those years also. During other years previous to 1928 I also enquired of some elderly Indian traders who annually go to Tarchen Mandi (Kailas) from Darma (Northern Almora). But none could tell me of any year in which they did not wade the Ganga Chhu and in which the bed of the Ganga Chhu was completely dry.

There are sufficient grounds to believe that a rise in the level of the water of Manasarovar and the consequent flow of water into Rakshas Tal through the Ganga Chhu make the flow continuous into the now so-called " Old bed of the Sutlej " from the Rakshas Tal. The rise of water in the Manasarovar and the consequent overflow into the Rakshas Tal through the Ganga Chhu may be caused not only by heavy rains but also by melting snow due to bright sunny days.

Manasarovar and Rakshas Tal might have been one continuous lake once and the range of hills now separating the two lakes might be due to a subsequent upheaval, the Ganga Chhu forming the outlet of Manasarovar into Rakshas Tal. This outlet is 40 to 100 feet in breadth and 2 to 4 feet in depth generally during the summer and rainy seasons. I took nine rounds of Manasarovar (out of which one was done in two days) and found the Ganga Chhu to be the only outlet of the Lake. So the statement and belief of several people who had never undertaken even one full circuit of Manasarovar, that the Brahmaputra takes its rise from Manasarovar on its eastern bank is absolutely groundless and untrue like the statements that the Indus has its source at the northern foot of Kailas and flows by its western side.

Old bed of the Sutlej: That part of the Sutlej where it is written on the Survey maps: " old bed of the Sutlej," contained water and there was continuous flow from Rakshas Tal up to Lejandak which is a day's march. I noticed it in August 1928 and also in August 1935. So the word " old bed of the Sutlej " should be deleted from the Survey maps, in view of the fact that there has been a continuous flow of water from the Manasarovar into the Rakshas Tal through the Ganga Chhu and from the Rakshas Tal into the now so-called " old bed of the Sutlej." Even taking for granted that the Ganga Chhu or the so-called " old bed of the Sutlej " becomes dry on some rare occasions in the course of a century, we cannot call that portion, from the Rakshas Tal to Lejandak, an " old bed of the Sutlej." Moreover

Sven Hedin himself writes, " Worthy of notice is the circumstance that according to the lamas of Tirthapuri the Sutlej came from Rakshas Tal...... Hence it seems that the monks trace back the Sutlej to Rakshas Tal, inspite of climatic variations which cause the water to fail periodically."

I do not know why and with what meaning and significance the Survey maps write " old bed of the Sutlej " from Rakshas Tal to Lejandak (in blue dashes) and " dry channel " from Lejandak to Dulchu (in black line) and yet keep the source of the Sutlej in the Kanglung glaciers. In all probability the Survey of India Office might have borrowed the nomenclature from Sven Hedin.

Ganges-Sutlej Confusion : For several generations there has been a hopeless confusion of the rivers Ganges and Sutlej, which is mainly two-fold. Most of the Western as well as the Eastern explorers, surveyors, tourists, and pilgrims to the Manasarovar lakes prior to Sven Hedin were under the wrong notion that the Ganges and the Sutlej took their rise from Manasarovar and Rakshas Tal, while some have confounded the Ganges with the Sutlej or made one the tributary of the other.

Hindu *Puranas* describe the Ganges as descending from the Mount Kailas. Isbrants Ides (1704) was informed by Jesuits in Piking, who in turn got the news from Chinese sources, that the Manasarovar and Rakshas Tal gave birth to the Ganges. Desideri (1715 A.D.) describes the Ganges as taking its rise in the Kailas and Manasarovar. Father Gaubil (1729) says that three head-streams of the Ganges flow into the Manasarovar. D'Anville (1735) makes the Langchen Khambab (Sutlej) identical with the Ganges. Father Joseph Tiffenthaler (1765?) confuses the Ganges with the Sutlej. Purangir, who accompanied Bogle and Turner to Tibet (1773) reports that the Ganges has its source on Kailas and from there it flows into the Manas and from the Manas it flows out again. Major J. Rennell (1782) describes the Ganges as running out of Manasarovar. Captain F. Wilford (1800) writes that the Ganges is the only river that really issues from Manasarovar. The source of the Ganges was finally discovered to be at Gangotri (Goumukh) in 1808 by Lieutenant Webb ; yet Webber (1866) placed the source of the Ganges on the southern flank of Gurla Mandhata ; and Ekai Kawaguchi, the Japanese Buddhist monk, who travelled through India and Tibet in 1897-1903, ' drank deep of the sacred water of the Ganga at the spring Chhumik Thungtol ' on the south-eastern side of Manasarovar, and made the Sutlej a tributary of the Ganges ! I need not mention the names of the several pious Hindu pilgrims, who still believe that the Ganges takes its rise from Manasarovar.

But up till now none, not even Sven Hedin, has explained satisfactorily why such a confusion was made repeatedly even by great explorers and writers. Certainly there must be some reason which has all along misled so many people into making such incorrect statements. Even to-day many orthodox and religious-minded Hindus as well as the cultured Indians confound the channel Ganga Chhu (the outlet of Manasarovar into Rakshas Tal) with

Ganga (River Ganges),* as the word 'Ganga' is common in both and say that "like the Indus, the Brahmaputra, the Saraju and the Sutlej, the Ganges (the third biggest of the Himalayan rivers) also has its source in Manasarovar," though the Ganges has absolutely no connection whatsoever with the River Ganges. No doubt, one Captain F. Wilford was about to point out the root cause of all the confusion when he quoted the Tibetan scripture thus: "the four sacred rivers, springing from the Manasarovara according to the divines of Tibet, are the Brahma-putra, the Ganges, the Indus and the Sita. The Ganges is the only one that really issues from the lake, and if the three others do it must be through subterranean channels; and such communications whether real or imaginary are very common in the Puranas."† Evidently the Captain was citing the passage from the Tibetan *Kailas Purana*. But most unfortunately the passage was quoted wrongly in part. Sven Hedin also quotes from the translation of some Tibetan works the four rivers Ganges, Sindu, Pakshu, and Sita as coming from the mountains with faces respectively of an elephant, a garuda, a horse, and a lion; but the courses of these rivers are not described in the commentary as in the *Kangri Karchhak*.

The real solution is very simple, provided one has a chance of having a glance into the *Kangri*

* 'Ganges' is the corrupted English form of the original Sanskrit word *Ganga*. *Ganga* is the common household term for 'Ganges' throughout India.

† Captain F. Wilford, quoted by Sven Hedin in his 'Trans-Himalaya,' Vol. III, p. 209.

Karchhak. Ganga, Sindhu, Sita and Pakshu or Vakshu are the Indian names, as given by the *Kangri Karchhak* to the Langchen Khambab (Sutlej), the Mapcha Khambab (Karnali), the Singi Khambab (Indus), and the Tamchok Khambab (Brahmaputra) respectively. Secondly Hardwar is called Chomo Ganga* by Tibetans. Thirdly, the Sutlej has been described as taking its source on the west of Manasarovar and flowing towards the west in Tibet and in India for some distance. It is further described as having taken a turn towards the east, flowing north of Buddha-Gaya and finally falling into the ocean on the east. It is on the support of these three points that Tibetans believe the Ganga Chhu and consequently the Sutlej to be the same as the Gages at Hardwar. Or it is also just possible that based on this wrong and confounded understanding the above statements about the Sutlej have been recorded in the *Kangri Karchhak*. Anyway there is undoubtedly a confusion of names and notions which requires clarification.

So it is the word 'Ganga Chhu' which has misled the Indians and the early explorers and writers to believe that the Ganges has its source in the Manasarovar; and it is the Indian equivalent 'Ganga' for the Sutlej in the *Kangri Karchhak*, which has misled Tibetans to believe that the Ganges at Hardwar is the same as the Ganga Chhu and consequently the Sutlej. It is these wrong

* *Chomo means 'nun:' so Chomo Ganga means Ganga-Mayi* of the Hindus or 'Mother Ganges' in English. The Ganges at Hardwar is also called *Chhumo* (big river) *Ganga*.

notions prevailing amongst the Indians and Tibetans that have to a great extent influenced and misled the various explorers, surveyors, travellers, pilgrims, and geographers up till now. I fervently hope that this piece of useful information will throw a flood of light on the subject and give a death-blow to the Ganges-Sutlej confusion which has been perpetuated for so many centuries.

CHAPTER III

SOURCE OF THE INDUS

Regarding the source of the Indus, Sven Hedin writes, " Our camping ground on the bank of the Indus (16,663 feet) is called Singi-buk. Eastwards the valley is broad and open but the Indus itself is here an insignificant stream. I was therefore not astonished when I heard that it is only a short day's journey to the source, which, I was told, does not proceed from snow or a glacier, but springs up out of the ground. The men called the river the Singi-tsangpo, or Singi-kamba, and the source itself Singi-kabab."*

" A little later we camp at the aperture of the spring, which is so well concealed that it might easily be overlooked without a guide."†

" At this point, the situation which had been discussed and searched for during some 2,000 years, the famous Singi-kamba or Indus is born. *But the infant river which is a mere brook, is much shorter than both the Lungdep and the Munjam.* Continuing north-eastwards one still remains for a considerable distance within the drainage area of

* 'Trans-Himalaya,' Vol. II, p. 210.
† *Op. cit.*, p. 212.

the Indus, for in fact and strictly hydrographically the Singi-kamba is only a right or northern tributary to the Bokhar-tsangpo, which, itself, is only a very insignificant brook. *Compared with the latter, both Lungdep and Munjam have a greater quantity of water and may be somewhat larger than the Bokhar*, though all of them are very short. From a hydrographic point of view *it may be said to be a matter of taste which of these different brooks should be regarded as the principal source of the Indus*. The question is of no great consequence, for, whichever branch should be chosen, its source is situated at a short day's march from the Singi-kabab. *The problem cannot be settled in any more satisfactory way than to accept the Tibetan view and regard the Singi-kabab as the source of the Indus, inspite of its being the shortest and one of the smallest of the several source branches. Any attempt to persuade the Tibetans that the Singi-kabab were not the real source would fail, for it has tradition in its favour*, is a sacred place adorned with *mani* pyramids and prayer stones, and it is one of the four famous kababs."*

" The velocity of the Singi-kampa was twice as great as that of the Gartong-chu. The volume of the Singi-kampa was 9·28 cubic metres per second, that of the Gartong-chu 6·67......Having decided that the Singi-kampa must be regarded as issuing from the true source of the Indus, Sven Hedin, followed this main branch of the river to its origin in the Trans-Himalaya. The first branch

*' Southern Tibet,' Vol. II, p. 213.

30. Kanglung Kangri Glaciers [See page 108

31. Chiu Hill, with Ganga Chhu flowing at its foot [See page 119

32. Singi Khambab [*See pages 81, 129*

33. Mapcha Chungo [*See page 134*

junction that he reached was that of Lungdep-chu : he found that there was a greater volume of water in the Lungdep-chu than in the Singi itself, and he was inclined to regard it as the source of the Indus, but as it was held by the local Tibetans to be a tributary only, he accepted their view, and persevered in climbing the rocky bed of the Singi. The volume of water in the next tributary the Munjam flowing into the Singi-kampa was very small (one-third of a cubic metre), and Sven Hedin continued his climb to the particular source, which the Tibetans called the source of the Singi-kampa. The source is known as the Singi-kabab, ' the Lion's mouth ' and is 16,941 feet high."*

Instead of first measuring the velocity of the two rivers, the Singi† Khambab and the Gartong chhu, at their confluence, and then going up the Singi Khambab to find out the sources of the Indus, as described to us by Burrard, Sven Hedin first fixed the source of the Indus in the Singi Khambab springs and then went down to measure the velocity of the water in the Gartong chhu. It was an accidental coincidence that the Singi Khambab carried more water than the Gartong at that time. Even if he had found Gartong chhu carrying more water, as it does oftentimes, Sven Hedin would certainly not have shifted his source from the Singi Khambab. Even taking for granted for a moment that Sven Hedin measured at first the velocities of the two rivers at the confluence and

* Burrard and Hayden, *op. cit.*, p. 241.

† Also pronounced ' Sengi ' or ' Senge.'

found the Singi Khambab carrying greater quantity of water than the Gartong and then went up the Singi Khambab to trace the source of the Indus, why should he miserably fail to apply this very "theory of greater quantity of water" only after a few days' march, and jump at the "tradition theory," when he reached the very first branch junction namely, the Lungdhep? But the great explorer completely overlooked the traditions of the local Tibetans when he went to fix the source of the Brahmaputra!

Both the Lungdhep chhu and the Munjan chhu which flow into the Singi, and the Bokhar chhu into which the tiny brook of the Singi Khambab springs flows are all decidedly several times bigger than the little brook formed by the springs of the Singi Khambab. Inspite of that Sven Hedin is liberal enough to give over-weightage to the Tibetan traditions for "the problem cannot be settled,......." The fact is, Sven Hedin could not spare more time for exploration in the circumstances under which he had to labour due to the restrictions of the Tibetan Government.

Of the different source streams of the Indus—the Tsethi chhu, the Lungdhep chhu, the Munjan chhu, and the Bokhar chhu, the Lungdhep chhu carries most water and is the longest of all the streams. I went to the source of the Indus by the Lhe la and returned by the Topchhen la; therefore I did not see personally the Tsethi chhu, but my guide informed me that the Lungdhep chhu is bigger than the Tsethi chhu. Next come the Munjan and the Bokhar chhu, both of which appeared to be almost of the same size; some shepherds held the Bokhar to be bigger than the Munjan, and my guide said that the Munjan was bigger than the Bokhar, but I am not definite about it. Anyway, the Lungdhep chhu is certainly the biggest and the longest, and as such its source, which is in the Topchhen la, should be considered the source of the Indus if the quantity of water or length is taken as criterion for fixing its source. The statement of some writers that the Indus takes its rise from the northern foot of the Kailas peak is absolutely wrong.

In spite of the overwhelming evidence to the contrary, Sven Hedin seeks to show that the credit of having discovered the sources of the Indus, Brahmaputra, and Sutlej goes to him as could be seen from the following passages.

"But no pundit had succeeded in penetrating to the source, and the one who had advanced nearest to it, namely, to a point 30 miles from it, had been attacked by robbers and forced to turn back. Consequently, until our time the erroneous opinion prevailed that the Indus had its source on the north flank of Kailas, and, *thanks to those admirable robbers, the discovery of the Indus source was reserved for me and my five Ladakis.*

"......*and I revelled in the consciousness that, except the Tibetans themselves, no other human beings but myself had penetrated to this spot. Great obstacles had been placed in my way, but Providence had secured for me the triumph of reaching the actual sources of the Brahmaputra and Indus, and ascertaining the origin of these two* historical rivers......Not without pride, but still with a feeling of humble thankfulness, I stood there, *conscious that I was the first white man who had ever penetrated to the sources of the Indus and Brahmaputra.*"* "*I loved this stream (Sutlej), for no white man had ever seen its source before now.*"†

Had Sven Hedin gone to the confluence of the Gartong and the Singi in summer, before visiting the Singi Khambab, he would have certainly found the water in the former to be greater than in the latter and would have fixed the source of the Indus at the head of the Gartong according to the quantity of water and he would never have cared either for the Singi Khambab or the Tibetan traditions and sentiments. Certainly the Gartong oftentimes carries more water than the Singi itself. However he found the water in the Singi to be greater than in the Gartong when he went there in early winter and remarked thus: "Accordingly the Singi-kamba, the Lion river is not only the longer but also the more voluminous of the two head-streams, and the problem is solved. Certainly it may be suggested that the dimensions given above only apply to late autumn and winter, for in summer and especially during the rainy season very different conditions may prevail. No doubt this is the case. The rainfall diminishes north-eastwards, and therefore more rain falls in the basin of the Gartong than in that of the Singi-kamba, which may be robbed of moisture by the Trans-Himalaya. The spring

* 'Trans-Himalaya,' Vol. II, pp. 212-214.
† 'Trans-Himalaya,' Vol. III, pp. 244, 245.

flood consequent on the melting of snow is also greater in the Gartong. How often irregularities must occur in consequence of the direction of the wind and capricious variations of temperature. In the mean time we may consider it probable that the Gartong carries during the whole year more water than the Singi-kamba, but *we have at least discovered that the Singi-kamba is a large stream, when no disturbing influences are at work, when there is no precipitation, and when the temperature in the two river basins may be considered identical.*"* The conditions mentioned in the passage are not often fulfilled except for a couple of months or so in the year. So should the quantity of water be taken into consideration, perhaps, the Gartong† may take the prominent place, yet to be thoroughly investigated by future explorers. But if the Tibetan traditions are taken into account the source of the Indus would be in the springs of Singi Khambab only.

The confusion of the Indus with the Sutlej (Langchen Khambab or Elephant-mouthed river) by several explorers in the past is perhaps due to the fact that the uppermost head-stream of the river Gartong (which is itself one of the headwaters of the Indus) is called Langpochhe chhu (Elephant-river).

* ' Trans-Himalaya, Vol. III, pp. 45, 46.

† I saw the source of the Gartong chhu (which is at the head of the Langpochhe chhu) from a distance of a few miles on September 19, 1928.

CHAPTER IV

Source of the Karnali

After two days' march from Taklakot up the Karnali, the fourth of the series of the four great rivers of the Holy Manasarovar, I reached a place called Mapcha Chungo on the right bank of the river. At the edge of the bank is a big *mani*-wall with several *mani*-slabs and streamers. Getting down a few yards towards the bed of the river I was shown the big spring of Mapcha Chungo (peacock head) gushing out from the wall of the steep bank of the river. I visited this place on September 9, 1928, and on August 23, 1936. There are some *mani*-stones and a few streamers near the spring. The water gushing out of the spring flows down a beautiful green velvety moss (having some resemblance to the neck of a peacock) into the Karnali below. This spring is the traditional source of the Map chhu or Mapcha Khambab (peacock-mouthed river or Karnali) and as such the actual or genetic source of the Map chhu or Karnali is near the Lampiya pass, wherefrom the main stream of the Karnali comes.

Some explorers have placed the source of the Karnali in the Rakshas Tal, because one of its head-streams, the Gurla chhu, has its source in the glaciers on the north-western slopes of the Gurla

Mandhata peaks, south-east of Gurla pass. This Gurla chhu flows into the Karnali, about a mile down the village Kardung. Those who go to Kailas by the Lipu Lekh pass and Taklakot, cross this stream at the southern foot of the Gurla pass. There is another small stream which has got its source on the south-eastern side of the Gurla pass (not very far from where Gurla chhu takes its rise) but flows to the northern side of the Gurla pass into Rakshas Tal. The Gurla chhu is a big stream whereas the other stream is a very small one. Those who did not trace the courses of the two streams closely, confounded both and placed the source of the Karnali (Mapcha Khambab) either in Rakshas Tal or in the Gurla Mandhata. The Gurla chhu is much smaller than the Map chhu proper. Moreover the traditional spring source—Mapcha Chungo—is on the Map chhu, which is the longest as well as the biggest headwater of the Karnali. So the glacial source of the Karnali is near Lampiya pass in the Zanskar range.

It may be noted that the combined river of Kali, coming from the Lipu Lekh pass and the Saraju coming from the Nandakot is called Sarada from Tankpur downwards. The Karnali coming from the Mapcha Chungo, ofter its mountainous course in Manasa Khanda and Nepal, is called Gogra, which receives the Sarada at Chouka ghat. From Chouka ghat till it falls into the Ganges, down Chapra, the combined river is known by both the names of Gogra and Saraju. I make a mention of this fact here, because some people believe that the river Saraju takes its rise from Manasarovar.

CONCLUSION

Traditional Sources : If Tibetan traditions are taken into account to fix the sources of the rivers under discussion, the source of the Sutlej (Langchen Khambab) is in the springs near Dulchu gompa,* about 22 miles west of Parkha ;† that of the Indus (Singi Khambab) is in the springs of Singi Khambab (half a mile north of Bokhar chhu), north-east of Kailas, 53 miles from Parkha ; the source of the Brahmaputra (Tamchok Khambab) is at the head of the Chema-yungdung at the Tamchok Khambab Chhorten, 92 miles from Parkha ; and that of the Karnali (Mapcha Khambab) is in the spring Mapcha Chungo, about 23 miles north-west of Taklakot.

When once it has been accepted that the sources of the Tibetan rivers are to be located according to the local tradition I have no dispute in accepting the source of the Indus, as pointed out by Sven Hedin, since I too came to the same conclusion when I visited the place on July 4, 1937, and stayed in the

* I visited Dulchu gompa on August 30, 1936, and the Kanglung glaciers on June 16, 1937.

† Distances are given from Parkha, as it is the Post-stage and Tibetan Official Transport Agency, situated midway between Kailas and Manasarovar. Mileages given in Tibetan area are subject to slight corrections.

surroundings for three days. But I would certainly make an emphatic note of dissent against his placing the sources of the Sutlej and the Brahmaputra in the Kanglung and the Kubi glaciers instead of in the traditional places, Dulchu gompa and the Chema-yungdung kangri glaciers respectively. If any other theory but that of tradition is accepted in fixing the sources of these rivers, the sources of all the three rivers, the Sutlej, the Indus, and the Brahmaputra are to be certainly shifted from their present positions as given by Sven Hedin and should be placed elsewhere after a fresh, systematic, and scientific exploration.

It will not be out of place if I quote here a few lines from the *Journal* of the Royal Geographical Society, London for February 1939, from T. G. Longstaff's note on my short paper on the subject published in the *Journal* : " I am in full agreement with him (Swami Pranavānanda) in accepting the traditional sources of the four rivers. If length is to be the criterion, then further survey is required. If volume is taken as the test, then, with glacial sources and an Arctic winter climate to contend with, flow must be measured throughout the year. It savours of impertinence for Europeans to assert their views against the usage of other civilizations."

I have got no objection if these rivers are traced to the genetic sources without dislocating the traditional places, as it is logical and does not tamper with the religious susceptibilities and usages of the local people concerned. Thus without dislocating the traditional sources we can trace to the genetic source, in the case of the Sutlej, either to the Lhe la or Tsethi la, (30 miles from Parkha) the head of the Lha chhu (according to the quantity of water); or to the Kanglung kangri glaciers (about 65 miles from Parkha), at the head of the Tag tsangpo (according to length). So also the genetic source of the Brahmaputra can be taken to the Chema-yungdung kangri glacier (or Tamchok Khambab kangri glaciers) a mile up the Tamchok Khambab Chhorten; and the genetic source of the Karnali to the Lampiya pass (two short days' journey from the traditional source, Mapcha Chungo), both in respect of length and volume of water. Then in the case of all these three rivers—Sutlej, Brahmaputra, and Karnali—the sources shall be glacial. But in the case of Indus if we want to go to the genetic source, without disturbing the traditional source, it would be at the head of the Bokhar chhu or near the Lama la (a short day's march from the springs of Singi Khambab), neither of which is glacial. Moreover the Bokhar chhu is neither the biggest nor the longest of the head-streams of the Singi.*

Sources according to the Quantity of Water: Should the quantity of water be the criterion, then the source of the Sutlej is near the Darma pass (four days' journey from Dulchu gompa), at the head of

It will not be out of place if I just make a reference here to the source of the river Kali. The genetic source of the Kali is near the Lipu Lekh pass, but the traditional source is in the springs of Kalapani, nine miles before reaching the Lipu Lekh. As the river Kali is considered the boundary between Nepal and British India, the territory of Nepal along the Kali ends abruptly at Kalapani. So it is clear that in the case of the Kali also, the traditional source in the springs of Kalapani has been accepted by the Survey Office and the British Government.

the river Darma yankti; the source of the Indus is near the Topchhen la (26 miles from Parkha) at the head of the Lungdhep chhu; the source of the Brahmaputra is in the Kubi glaciers at the head of the Kubi river (3 or 4 short days' march from the Chema-yungdung glaciers); and the source of the Karnali is near the Lampiya pass (2 short days' march from the spring Mapcha Chungo). When thus volume is taken into consideration the sources are all glacial. Excepting in the case of the Karnali, the traditional sources of all the other three rivers are dislocated. According to volume the source of the Sutlej may also be either at the head of the Trokpo-shar chhu, or at the head of the Chukta chhu, or at the head of the Lha chhu, which has been already discussed in detail under the heading "Source of the Sutlej."

Sources according to the Length: Should length be the test, the source of the Sutlej would be in the Kanglung kangri. But the Samo tsangpo and the southern tributary (Ganga) of the Tag should also be given due consideration which, I was informed by some nomads recently, are longer than the Tag and which neither Sven Hedin nor I did investigate by going to their sources. It may be remembered that the word 'Ganga' is a synonym of 'Sutlej' in Tibetan scriptures. The source of the Indus would be near the Topchhen la at the head of the Lungdhep chhu; the source of the Brahmaputra is in the Chema-yungdung or Tamcok Khambab kangri glaciers at the head of the river Chema-yungdung; and the source of the Karnali is near the Lampiya pass. When length is taken as the test, the traditional sources of the three rivers—Sutlej, Brahmaputra, and Karnali—are in tact, and that of the Indus alone is dislocated; but the sources of all the rivers are glacial.

Sven Hedin's sources of the Sutlej in the Kanglung kangri, of the Indus in the springs of Singi Khambab, and of the Brahmaputra in the Kubi glaciers would not satisfy any one of the above three criteria—tradition, volume, or length—in its entirety; and as such he cannot claim to be "the first white man and European" to discover the sources of these rivers finally, unless one accepts his fixing of the sources at random, applying different criteria for different rivers, to suit his own convenience, whim, and taste.

I now leave the matter for serious consideration to the earnest and sincere seekers after truth in this realm of knowledge to draw their own judgment in the light of the few facts I have placed before them. Truth will and shall have to come to light some day. It cannot be hidden for ever.

Let me close my thesis with the famous quotation from the *Brihadaranyaka Upanishad*:

असतो मा सद्गमय
तमसो मा ज्योतिर्गमय
मृत्योर्माऽमृतं गमय ॥

From untruth lead me to Truth;
From darkness lead me to Light;
From mortality lead me to Immortality.

ॐ

APPENDIX I

GLOSSARY OF TIBETAN AND OTHER WORDS

[H.—Hindi; S.—Sanskrit; the rest are Tibetan words.]

Bhot (H.)—Indian borderland of North Almora, North Garhwal, North Tehri, etc.

Bhotia (H.)—People of Bhot.

Bodhisattva (S.)—One who could have attained *Nirvana* but has delayed it and has remained in the world to help the striving human beings and preach the Law.

Both or Po—Tibet.

Chaktak—Chain.

Chema—Sand.

Chema-nenga—Five sands.

Chenresi—Avalokiteswara.

Chhak-chhal-gang—A place wherefrom prostration salute is made.

Chhanadorje or Chhagnadorje—Vajrapani.

Chhang—A kind of light beer made by fermenting barley.

Chhansu—Tax-Collector.

Chhorten—A sort of monument corresponding to a *stupa*.

Chhu—Water, river, rivulet, or stream.

Chhura—Cheese.

Chomo—Nun.

Daba—Ordinary monk.

Dalai Lama—Ocean-monk; the Sovereign, spiritual, and political head of Tibet, believed to be the incarnation of the Bodhisattva Avalokiteswara.

Dama—A sort of thorny bush, which is used as fuel and which burns even when green.

Damaru (S.)—Vibrant drum.

Dema—Tibetan cow.

Donkhang—*Dharmashala* or traveller's bungalow or rest house.

Garpon—Viceroy.

Gompa or gonpa—Buddhist monastery.

Gopa or goba—Village headman.

Gormo—Rupee.

Havan (S.)—Offerings to the fire.

Huniya (H.)—Tibetan.

Jambyang—Manjusree.

Jav—Half a *tanga*.

Jhabbu—Cross-breed of Tibetan bull and Indian cow.

Jinbu—Tibetan onion plant.

Joo—Salutation or thanks.

Kangri or gangri—Glacier.

Kangri Karchhak—*Kailas Purana.*

Kang Rinpochhe—Holy Kailas.

Kanjur—Translation of Buddha's sayings and teachings.

Khamjam-bho—Salutation.

Khampa—Tibetan domiciled in India, or a native of Kham—a province in Eastern Tibet.

Khatak—Loosely woven gauze-like white linen used in lieu of a garland.

Kiyang—Wild horse.

Kora—Circumambulation.

Korlo—Prayer-mill.

La—Pass.

Lama—Guru, Buddhist monk of higher order.

Langak Tso—Rakshas Tal or Ravan Hrad.

Langchen Khambab—Elephant-mouthed river or the Sutlej.

Laptche—A heap of stones generally raised at the end of ascents, wherefrom some holy place is seen first, or at the top of passes, or on the way to any holy place.

Lham—Tibetan shoes coming up to the knees.

Magpon—Patwari.

Mandi (H.)—Market or mart.

Mani—The *mantra, Om ma ni pad me hum.*

Mantra (S.)—Mystic formula.

Mapcha Khambab or Map chhu—Peacock-mouthed river or the Karnali.

Mapham—Manasarovar, the unconquerable.

Mavang—Manasarovar, the un-enslaved.

Mayur—Fissure.

Ngangba—Swan.

Ngari—Western Tibet.

Nirvana (S.)—Salvation.

Phuk—Cave.

Prasad (S.)—Something taken from a holy place as a sacred memento.

Puja (S.)—Worship.

Purana (S.)—A book of Hindu Mythology.

Rinpochhe—Holiness, jewel, or holy.

Sattu (H.)—Parched barley powder.

Siddha (S.)—One who has attained high psychic and supernatural powers.

Singi Khambab—Lion-mouthed river or the Indus.

Tanga or tanka—Silver coin, equivalent to $\frac{1}{3}$ of a rupee.
Tanjur—Translation of all *Shastras*.
Tantricism (S.)—Mystic cult.
Tarchok—Coloured flags or festoons of rags.
Tasam—High road.
Tasam, Tazam, or Tarzam—Post-stage or Transport Office or Officer.
Thanga—Plateau.
Thanka—A banner-painting hung in monasteries.
Thukpa—Semi-liquid dish made out of *tsampa*.
Thuma—A rejuvenating medical herb.
Tsampa or tsamba—*Sattu* or parched barley powder.
Tsangpo—Big river, also used for the Brahmaputra.
Tso—Lake.
Tulku lama—Incarnation monk.

Urko Kong—Viceroy Senior.
Urko Yok—Viceroy Junior.

Yak—Tibetan bull.
Yankti (Bh.)—River.
Yantra (S.)—A mystic diagrammatic representation.
Yung Chhong—Tibetan Trade Agent or State Merchant.

Zong—Fort or Governor's residential place, or the Governor.

Zongpon—Governor.

APPENDIX II

ROUTES TO THE SOURCES OF THE FOUR RIVERS

TABLE I

Tarchen to the Source of the Indus by the Lhe la and back by the Topchhen la—92 miles

Halt No.	Name of place	Distance between two places	Total mileage	Remarks
	Tarchen* ...	0	0	Also pronounced Darchen; 15,100 ft., Parkha *Tasam* is 7½ m.† from here;
	Sershung ...	3¾		here is the flag-staff called *Tarbochhe*, dedicated to the Lord Buddha; cross the Lha chhu to its right bank to reach the gompa;
	Nyanri ...	1¼		also called Chhuku; first monastery of Kailas; there are two big elephant tusks in it; the cave Langchen-phuk is very near the monastery; about 5 m. farther the Dunglung chhu falls into the Lha chhu, upper part of the Dunglung valley abounds in wild yaks and one path goes up the valley to the Singi Khambab;

* Tarchen is a village situated at the southern foot of the *Kailas Parvat*, where Kailas *parikrama* both begins and ends. This village belongs to Bhutan State and is under a Bhutanese officer called Tarchen Labrang, who owns a big house. There are also a few huts and some black

† m. = mile or miles.

TABLE I—*continued*

Halt No.	Name of place	Distance between two places	Total mileage	Remarks
	Diraphuk gompa*	7¼		second monastery of Kailas, the best and the most imposing view of the Mount Kailas can be had from here; leave the *parikrama* route to the right and proceed northward up the Lha chhu; 3¼ m. to Selung-ma, 2⅛ m. to Chhulung-ma, 1⅛ m. to Kelung-ma, ¾ m. to
1	Dolungba ...	7¼	19½	Dolungva, C. G.,† very cold, from here very steep ascent to the pass,
	Lhe la ...	3½		also called Lapche Chikpa la, cairns, and *laptches*, steep descent to
	Sharshumi ...	5¼		C. G.,
	Lungdhep chhu ...	6		the stream coming from Lhe la falls into the Lungdhep,

tents. A Mandi is held here by the Bhotias of Johar and Darma Paraganas for over 2½ months every year. Provisions can be got from the Mandi. This is a big wool-shearing centre One can have a glimpse of the Kailas peak from here.

* There are three routes from Diraphuk to go to the Singi Khambab : (1) up the Dunglung chhu by the Dunglung la, (2) up the Lha chhu by the Tsethi and Tsethi-lachen la, and (3) by the Lhe la, which is the shortest of the three routes. The second route is a very bad and a long one, and the first is the longest. For returning to Tarchen from the Singi Khambab the route by the Topchhen la is the nearest and easiest. Tibetan Pilgrims to the Singi Khambab follow the route given in this table because in so doing they can do the circuit of the Holy Kailas avoiding the steep ascent and descent of the Dolma la. The author took eight rounds of the Holy Kailas.

† C. G.=Camping ground.

TABLE I—*continued*

Halt No.	Name of place	Distance between two places	Total mileage	Remarks
2	Lungdhep camp ...	2¼	36½	C. G. on either side of the river, black tents, (about a mile down this place, situated on the right bank of the river is the hill Lungdhep-Ningri, at the foot of which the river is formed into a big lake, called Lungdhep-Ningri tso), cross the thigh-deep river to its right bank, after some ups and downs to
	Rungmagem camp* ...	7½		C. G., blank tents, ¾ m. very steep ascent, ¾ m, very steep descent to Bokhar chhu, ½ m. farther up to
3	SINGI KHAMBAB† ...	2	46	Singi Khambab or the Source of the Indus, C. G., 16,950 ft., black tents in the surroundings,

* The upper course of the river is called Munjan chhu, and the lower course Rungmagem chhu till it joins the Singi or the Indus. There are hundreds of yaks and thousands of sheep and goats, in this region of the Singi, belonging to the shepherds of Amdo. There are extensive pasture-lands here. The dairy products of these regions are considered the best in the whole of Tibet. One may start good Dairy Farms here with great advantage.

† Here are three or four fresh water springs welling up out of the ground. Near by is a quadrangular *mani*-wall with several *mani*-stones. Thre are some stones over 1½ feet high each containing a single letter of the *mani-mantra*. On another stone the wheel of Law (*Dharma Chakra*) is inscribed. The temperature of the combined waters of the

TABLE I—*continued*

Halt No.	Name of place	Distance between two places	Total mileage	Remarks
	Rungmagem ...	2		C. G.,
	Lungdhep- ... Ningri	4¼		C. G.,
	Lungdhep chhu	2		C. G.,
	Nyimalung chhu	4½		cross it to its left bank, this falls into the Lungdhep chhu, one furlong down below almost opposite the Lhe la chhu; 4 m. farther up the valley cross the kneedeep Lungdhep to its left bank, 3½ m. farther to
4	Foot of Topchhen la	7¼	66	C. G., very cold, from here very steep ascent on stones and through big boulders to
	Topchhen la ...	5	71	Topchhen la, 7 m. very steep descent on stones. 5 m. descent down the valley ; Kailas is seen from here, ¾ m. farther

springs was 48·5°F. The water coming out of the springs forms into weedy ponds and flows out into the Bokhar chhu as a small brook, half a mile down below. Just by the side of the springs, situated on the edge of a huge slab of white rock are three pillar-like *laptches*, and some *mani*-stones, on one of which were some coloured rags of cloth offered by some Tibetan pilgrims. The rugged hill on the north of the springs is called Singi-Yura and to the south situated on the left bank of the Bokhar chhu is Singi-Chava, crossing which one gets down to Rungmagem camp. To the north-east of the Singi Khambab is the Lama la. I visited the Source of the Indus on July 4, 1937, and stayed in the surroundings for three days. Singi is also pronounced as 'Sengi' or 'Senge'. Khambab is pronounced as 'Khamba' by the Eastern Tibetans.

TABLE I—*concluded*

Halt No.	Name of place	Distance between two places	Total mileage	Remarks
				is the confluence of the Topchhen chhu and the Lham-chhikhir, camps everywhere from Topchhen la to this place ; cross the thighdeep Lham-chhikhri chhu to its right bank, Kailas *parikrama* road, 1½ m. to
	Zunthulphuk gompa	14½		the third monastery of Kailas; there are two small elephant tusks in this gompa.
5	Tarchen ...	6½	92	

TABLE XI

Parkha to the Sources of the Brahmaputraan d the Tag and back to Taklakot by the Gurla la—193 miles

Halt No.	Name of place	Distance between two places	Total mileage	Remarks
	Parkha* ...	0	0	Also pronounced Barkha, 15,050 ft., Tarchen is 7½ m. from here,
1	Ngalukro ...	13	13	C. G., cross the Gyuma chhu and proceed, on the way to Seralung, cross the Palchen chhu and the Palchung chhu and the Samo tsangpo,
2	Seralung† ...	16	29	sixth monastery of Manasarovar, fine view of the Holy Lake,
3	Namarding ...	15	44	to Namarding *via* Chomokur, C. G., big camp, the Manas is seen from here,
				2 m. in the valley, ¾ m. ordinary ascent, 1¼ m. very steep ascent to

* Parkha is the third *Tasam* on Gartok-Lhasa high road. There are two houses here, one of which belongs to the *Tasam* and the other is a Rest House. There are also some black tents of shepherds where milk, curds, *chhura*, and butter may be purchased.

† The route from Tarchen to Seralung is as follows : Tarchen to Zhong chhu 3 m., to Avang chhu 2¾ m., Philung Kongma chhu 2m., Philung Pharma ½ m., Philung Yongma 2½ m., Gyuma chhu 2½ m.; Kyo camp ½ m., and Kuglung chhu 2½ m. (total 16 m., for the first day); Lungnak chhu 3¾ m., Kurkyal Chhungo begins 1½ m., (the lake is about 2¾ m. long), Palchen chhu 3¼ m., Palchung chhu 1¼ m., and Seralung gompa 6¼ m. (total 16 m., for the second day).

TABLE II—*continued*

Halt No.	Name of place	Distance between two places	Total mileage	Remarks
	Changsha la ...	4		Changsha la, 1½ m. very steep descent to a C. G.,
	Chhumik Thungtol*	3½		2 m. nearly to Chhumik Thungtol, sacred spring,
	Langchen Khambab	¾		the spring is marked by several cairns and a big *laptche* in which is fixed a small pole bedecked with pieces of coloured rags like a scarecrow, the spring flows through black boulders into the Tag that is near by; ¼ m. farther there are white sands on either bank and in the bed of the river Tag for about 2 m.;
4	Tagramochhe	2¾	55	big camps (from here one path goes up along the Tag tsangpo for about 10 m. to the KANGLUNG KANGRI, the Source of the Tag ;) 1 m. Tagramochhe chhu,
	Takkarbu la	2		1 m. to the la *laptche*, for 5¼ m. proceed on along boulders, stones, beds of sharp gravel, over ups and downs to

* *Chhu*=water, *mik*=eye, *thung*=see, *tol*=salvation or *Nirvana*; *i.e.*, whoever even sees this eye-like spring obtains salvation or *Nirvana*. The spring Chhumik Thungtol is situated in the deep valley of the Tag tsangpo, between high volcanic mountains. It is surrounded by a big quadrangular *mani*-wall 16 by 10 yards with flags and festoons (*tarchoks*) just overhanging the spring, which is 3 or 4 feet deep and 8 feet in diameter. Through the turquoise blue water, could be clearly seen the

TABLE II—*continued*

Halt No.	Name of place	Distance between two places	Total mileage	Remarks
	Chamar ...	5¼		Chamar, C. G., a hill on the left side of the road, on the top of the hill are some *tarchoks* and *laptches* (this hill is just opposite the Kang-lung glaciers), on the way are some small lakelets,
	Tag la ...	¾	63	17,382 ft., *laptches* and *tarchoks*,
	Tamlung tso	3½		this lake is called Brahma-kund by the Bhotias, extensive camps on the shores of the lake, there are also several other small lakelets connected with one another, 2½ m. parallel to the lake (a stream from this lake flows out into the Angsi chhu), 2½ m. farther one path goes eastward to Kong-yu tso, Bongba, etc., 2¼ m. gentle up towards the south, (Kongyu tso is seen from here on the north), 2¼ m. descent, steep descent, very steep descent, and descent to

blue and red beads, four inferior turquoises, two bangles, some shells and other petty articles, thrown in as offerings by pilgrims. The water in the spring is crystal clear and flows out from the bottom as a small brook into the Tag on its right bank a few yards below. The names of the three mountains between which the spring is situated are Chenresi (white), Chhagnadorje (blue), and Jambyang (yellow). There are several cairns on the way to the spring and further up.

TABLE II—*continued*

Halt No.	Name of place	Distance between two places	Total mileage	Remarks
5	Angsi chhu ...	9½	76	Angsi chhu, camps on either side of the river, cross the thighdeep river, the valley is full of lakelets, very broad and grand, good grass, ½ m. Angsi valley, 1¼ m. mild and steep ascent, nearly 2½ m. very gentle up on the plateau to
	Shibla Ringmo la	4¼		the pass, it is like a narrow lane between two steep beautiful mountains, *laptche* (in the middle of the plateau, on to the left and just near the pass are two lakelets of great depth, several herds of wild goats are seen, ¾ m. steep descent down a narrow gorge (on the left is a beautiful lakelet), 3¼ m. ups and downs on beds of stones, mid-way is a beautiful semi-circular lake with an island in the middle, some more lakelets, cross a stream, ½ m. farther ascent, 1½ m. very steep and dan-gerous descent to the

TABLE II—*continued*

Halt No.	Name of place	Distance between two places	Total mileage	Remarks
	Chema-yung-dung chhu	$5\frac{1}{2}$		Chema-yungdung chhu, the whole bed of the river and the right bank are full of white quartz, as if covered with snow; like the Angsi valley this velley also is full of lakelets,
	Chema-yungdung-pu	$5\frac{1}{2}$		first glacier of the Tam-chok Khambab ; huge debris and big land-slips are lodged at the tongue of the glacier ; there are more than one lakelet on the debris and the glacier.
6	TAMCHOK KHAMBAB	$\frac{3}{4}$	92	Tamchok Khambab or the Source of the Brahma-putra.
	Sibla Ringmo la	$11\frac{3}{4}$		

* Tamchok Khambab, the Horse-mouthed river takes its source here. Here is a big boulder about 12 feet high, on which are two foot-prints, over which is built a loose stone-walled hut facing the east. On the top of the hut are placed two horns of a wild yak. Adjacent to the boulder are one roofed and two unroofed *donkhangs* of loose stones piled up rudely. All around are several cairns. There is a dry spring near by which is said to contain water in summer and rainy seasons. The river Tamchok Khambab or Chema-yungdung, as called here, is 50 yards from the monument or *Chhorten.* One mile up this place is another big glacier which my guide said was the main glacier of Tamchok Khambab from which the Tamchok Khambab actually takes its rise. This and the Chema-yung-dung-pu glacier are the two ears of the Brahmaputra and go by the common name of Chema-yungdung-pu, or simply Chema-yungdung. It is also pro-nounced as 'Chema-yuntung' and 'Chema-yundung.' *Chema*=sand, *yuntung*=*Swastika*. Opposite the monument is a board-faced peak, separating the two glaciers. To the W. or N. W. of the main glacier of the Tamchok Khambab is another small glacier, behind which is the Angsi glacier. I visited the Source of the Brahmaputra on June 17 and 18, 1937, when the whole bed of the river 5 to 20 yards broad was frozen *en bloc* 6 to 7 feet thick for 3 miles beginning from the main glacier downwards. In the middle of the frozen bed of the river, a ditch-like stream was flowing beautifully 3 to 6 feet broad and about 6 feet

TABLE II—*continued*

Halt No.	Name of place	Distance between two places	Total mileage	Remarks
7	Angsi chhu ...	$4\frac{1}{4}$	108	C. G.,
	Tag la ...	13		17,382 ft.,
8	Tagramochhe...	8	129	C. G.,
	Chhumik ... Thungtol	$4\frac{1}{2}$		sacred spring, C. G., after $14\frac{1}{2}$ m. cross the thighdeep furious Tag to its left bank,
	Tomomopo ...	$15\frac{3}{4}$		$1\frac{1}{4}$ m. farther is Tomomopo, geysers and boiling hot springs, C. G.,
9	Tagpotong (?)...	$\frac{3}{4}$	150	C. G., several hot springs varying from luke warm to boiling temperature; a regular stream of hot water is flowing out of these hot water springs into the Tag. There are some more hot springs on the other side of the river opposite this place at Chhu-phuk and at Ambu-phuk, 1 m. beyond that place ; plenty of *jinbu* grows wild in the surroundings;
	Nimapendi ... chhu	$3\frac{1}{2}$		kneedeep, cross it to its left bank, in this valley there are about 25 black tents of Nonokur for the greater part of the year

deep, between the perpendicular ice-walls. Nyakora nomad shepherds go there in August for wild yak hunting, which is to be found in large numbers. Sven Hedin has wrongly placed the Source of the Brahmaputra in the Kubi glaciers instead of in the Chema-yungdung glaciers. There is plenty of good grass in the Chema-yungdung valley. The white sands of the river are very conspicuous for about ten miles from the source downwards, and they can be seen from long distances, as if there has been a fresh snowfall.

TABLE II—*concluded*

Halt No.	Name of Place	Distance between two places	Total mileage	Remarks
	Yerngo gompa	$8\frac{1}{4}$		seventh monastery of the Lake,
10	Thugolho* ...	$2\frac{1}{4}$	159	also called Thugu or Thokar, eighth and the most important of all the monasteries of the Holy Manasarovar, 2 m. to Namreldi chhu, $1\frac{1}{4}$ m. to Selung Hurdung chhu, $5\frac{1}{4}$ m. gradual ascent to
	Gurla la† ...	$9\frac{1}{2}$		big *laptches*, flags, festoons and cairns; 16,200 ft., steep descent to
	Gori udyar or Gurla phuk	4		C. G., caves,
11	Baldak ...	$4\frac{1}{2}$	177	big C. G., 15,000 ft.,
	Ringung ...	$4\frac{1}{2}$		village, C. G.,
	Toyo ...	$8\frac{1}{2}$		village, General Zoravar Sing's *samadhi*,
12	Taklakot ...	3	193	village, Zong, Similing monstery, Mandi, 13,100 ft.; Lipu Lekh pass, the Indian borderland is 11 m. from here.

* There are eight houses and two *donkhangs*. One can have a fine view of Kailas from here. It is in this monastery that the author lived during the years 1936-37 to do his Spiritual *Sadhana*. A decently big Mandi is held here in the months of July and August by the Bhotias of Byans, Chaudans, and Darma. This is a big wool-shearing centre.

† From here one can command a grand panoramic view of the surrounding region. On the back (in the south) is the long range of snow peaks beginning from the Kamet, Lipu Lekh to Nepal peaks; on to the right are the massive giant heads of the Gurla Mandhata (25, 355; 22, 650; 22, 160); and in the front are the crystal clear emerald-watered Holy Manas Lake and Rakshas Tal (on the right and left respectively), in the background of which stands aloof in the Kailas range. conspicuously and picturesquely the majestic silvery Kailas Dome with awe-inspiring solemnity and weired grandeur, facing the proud Mandhata and overlooking the twin lakes. Parkha is about 23 miles from here by the direct route.

TABLE III

Parkha to the Source of the Sutlej at Dulchu Gompa—22 miles

Halt No.	Name of Place	Distance between two places	Total mileage	Remarks
	Parkha ...	0	0	*Tsam*, ¼ m. farther cross the Dama chhu and in the course of 3 m. cross three ramifications of the Zhong chhu or Lha chhu,
	Lha chhu ...	3½		Cross the thighdeep Lha chhu, which is about 150 yards bread and very swift,
1	Loma-goma ...	6½	10	C. G., by the side of the so-called "old bed of the Sutlej",
	Changje-changju	3½		C. G., Gyanima-Tarchen road crosses,
2	DULCHU GOMPA*	8½	22	monastery and some black tents, several *mani*-walls; not far from the gompa are several springs of fresh water welling out of the ground which the Tibetans assert to be the traditional Source of the Langchen Khambab or the Sutlej. Tirthapuri (Tretapuri or Pretapuri in Tibetan) is about 15 m. from here.

* The Darma pass wherein lies the source of the Darma yankti (Langchen tsangpo) is at a distance of four days' journey from here.

TABLE IV

Taklakot to the Source of the Karnali at Mapcha Chungo—23 miles

Halt No.	Name of place	Distance between two places	Total mileage	Remaks
	Takalkot ...	0	0	Zong, monastery, Mandi, after 2½ m. cross the Karnali to
	Toyo ...	3		village, Zoravar Sing's *chhorten*,
	Delaling ...	¼		village, cross the Garu chhu,
	Ringung chhu	7¼		Before reaching this stream are the villages Ronam on the right and Salung and Doh situated on the right bank of the Map chhu,
	Map chhu or Karnali ...	¼		cross the thigh-deep river to its right bank,
1	Harkong ...	3½	14¼	village with 3 houses and some black tents,
	Pass ...	6¾		last ¾ m. steep ascent,
2	MAPCHA CHUNGO* ...	2	23	first ¾ m. very steep descent, traditional Source of Map chhu or the Karnali.

* Situated on the edge of the right bank of the Map chhu is a big *mani*-wall with several *mani*-slabs and streamers. Getting down a few yards towards the bed of the river is the big spring of Mapcha Chungo (Peacock-head) gushing out from the wall of the steep bank of the river. There are some *mani*-stones and a few streamers near the spring. The water gushing out of the spring flows down a beautiful green velvety moss (having some resemblance to the neck of the peacock) into the Map chhu below. The glacial source of the Karnali is near the Lampiya pass which is at a distance of two short days' march from here.

TABLE V

*Abstract of Mileage between Important Places in Kailas Khanda and Kedar Khanda**

						Miles
1.	Almora	to Kailas	*via*	Lipu Lekh	Pass	237
2.	,,	,,	,,	Darma	,,	233
3.	,,	,,	,,	Unta Dhura	,,	209
4.	Joshimath	,,	,,	Gunla-Niti	,,	202
5.	,,	,,	,,	Damjan-Niti	,,	163
6.	,,	,,	,,	Hoti-Niti	,,	160
7.	Badrinath	,,	,,	Mana	,,	240
8.	Mukhuva (Gangotri)	,,	,,	Jelukhaga	,,	245
9.	Simla	,,	,,	Shipki pass & Gartok		443
10.	,,	,,	,,	,, Tuling		475
11.	Srinagar (Kashmir)	,,	,,	Ladakh		603
12.	Pashupatinath (Nepal)	,,	,,	Muktinath & Khocharnath		525?
13.	Lhasa to Kailas					800?
14.	Kailas *Parikrama*					32
15.	Circumference of Manasarovar					54
16.	Kailas (Tarchen) to the Source of Indus *via* Lhe la or Topchhen la					46
17.	Parkha to the Source of Brahmaputra					92
18.	,, ,, ,,			Sutlej (at Dulchu gompa)		22
19.	,, ,, ,,			Tag		65
20.	Taklakot ,,	,,		Karnali		23
21.	Kailas	to		Manasarovar		16
22.	,,	,,		Tirthapuri		37
23.	,,	,,		Gyanima Mandi		40
24.	Tirthapuri	,,		,,		27
25.	Gyanima	,,		Gartok		76
26.	,,	,,		Sibchilim Mandi		28
27.	,,	,,		Taklakot		49

* This table was originally an inset in the map; but to give place to some other insets, this has to be printed as a separate table.

TABLE V—*concluded*

				Miles
28.	Taklakot	,,	Thugolho	34
29.	,,	,,	Khocharnath	12
30.	Sibchilim	,,	Nabra Mandi	38½
31.	Nabra Mandi	,,	Tuling	33½
32.	Tuling	,,	Badrinath	100?
33.	Badrinath	,,	Joshimath	19
34.	Haldwani	,,	Almora (on foot)	41
35.	,,	,,	,, (by bus)	83
36.	Almora	,,	Pindari Glacier	73
37.	Rishikesh	,,	Jamnotri	118½
38.	,,	,,	Gangotri	145
39.	,,	,,	Kedarnath	133½
40.	,,	,,	Badrinath	167½
41.	,,	,,	Joshimath	148½
42.	Ramnagar	,,	Badrinath	164
43.	Jamnotri	,,	Gangotri	98½
44.	Gangotri	,,	Kedarnath	123
45.	Kedarnath	,,	Badrinath	101
46.	Mussoori	,,	Jamnotri	86
47.	Gangotri	,,	Goumukh	13
48.	Uttarkashi	,,	Dodi tal	18
49.	Kedarnath	,,	Vasuki tal	2
50.	Chamoli	,,	Gohan	16
51.	Pandukeswar	,,	Lokpal	15
52.	Badrinath	,,	Satopanth	18
53.	Milam	,,	Shandilya kund	16
54.	Dharchula	,,	Chhiplakot	25
55.	Tarchen	,,	Sirdung Chuksum	7
56.	,,	,,	Tso Kapala	6

ADDENDUM

(*to page 52, line 28*)

In 1899 a big fire broke out in Khocharnath gompa and destroyed the two side-images of Avalokiteswara and Vajrapani. Later they were repaired by Nepalese sculptors. Another tradition says that all the three images along with the pedestal were brought to this monastery from Lanka or Ceylon.

8. EKAI KAWAGUCHI'S MAP

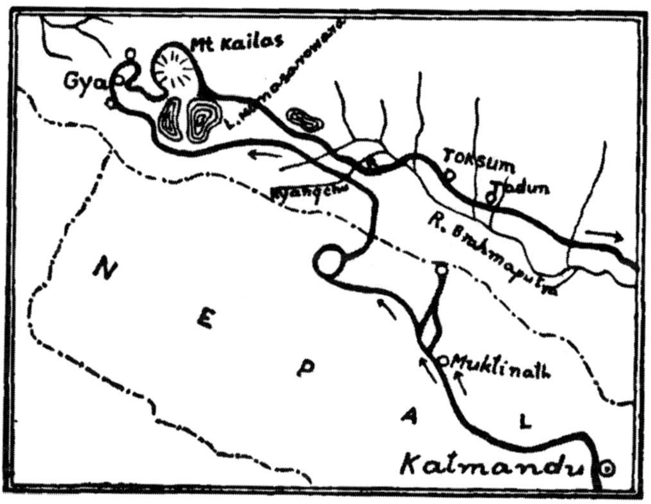

N.B. This sketch was originally intended to be the eighth inset in Map No. I. But, for want of room in the Map this has to be given here as a separate inset.

VARIOUS ROUTES TO THE HOLY KAILĀS & MĀNASARŌVAR

EXPLORATION IN TIBET — MAP NO. I

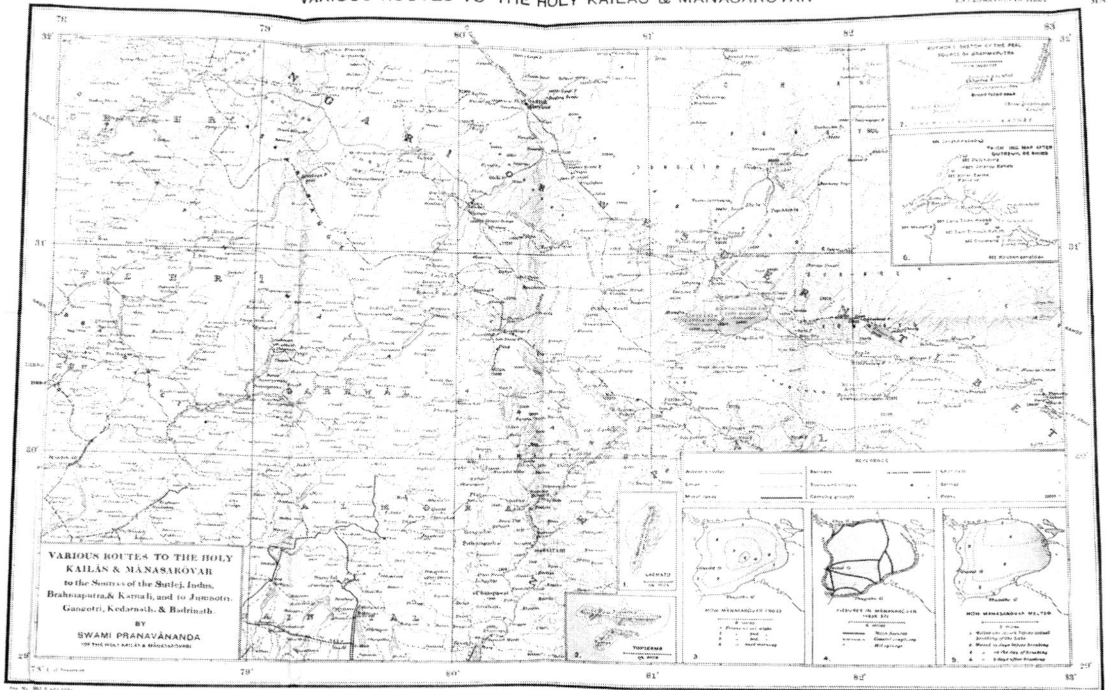

Based on Survey of India maps with the permission of the Surveyor General.

THE HOLY KAILĀS AND MĀNASARŌVAR

MAP NO. II
EXPLORATION IN TIBET

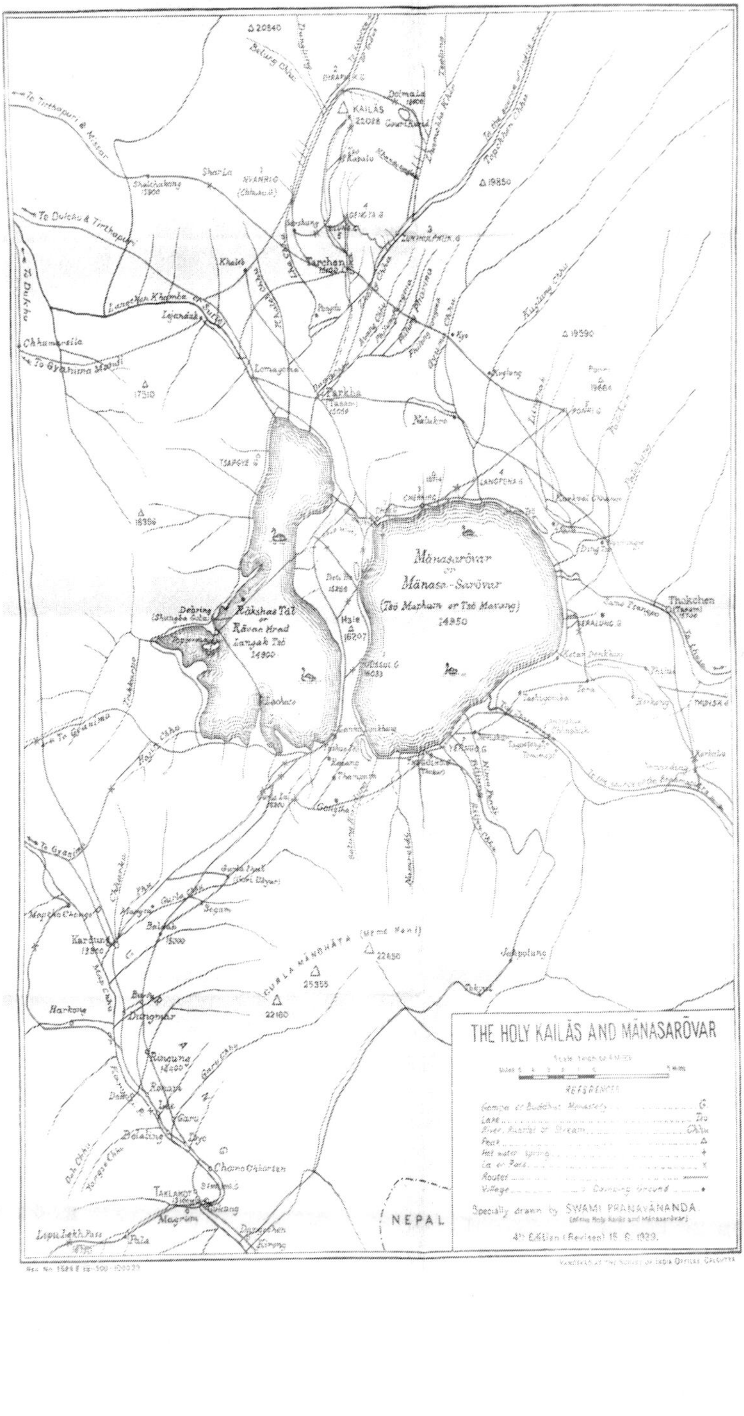